Teaching Drama
to Young Children

Mem Fox

Teaching Drama to Young Children

Illustrated by Bob Graeme

Heinemann
Portsmouth, New Hampshire

For Jane Juttner,
who took Chloë sailing

Heinemann
A Division of Reed Publishing (USA) Inc.
361 Hanover Street, Portsmouth, NH 03801-3912
Offices and agents throughout the world

First United States edition © 1987 by Mem Fox. First
published in 1984 under the title *How to Teach Drama
to Infants (Without Really Crying!)* by Ashton Scholastic
Pty Limited (Inc. in NSW), P.O. Box 579, Gosford 2250,
Australia.

Library of Congress Cataloging-in-Publication Data

Fox, Mem, 1946–
   Teaching drama to young children.

   Previously published as: How to teach drama to
infants (without really crying!). 1984.
   Includes bibliographical references.
   1. Drama in education.   2. Drama—Study and
teaching (Primary)   I. Title.
PN3171.F69   1986   372.6'6'07   86-14858
ISBN 0-435-08265-5

Designed by Wladislaw Finne.
Illustrated by Bob Graeme.
Printed in the United States of America.

10   9   8   7   6   5   4

Contents

Introduction 1

Section I: Song and Dance 7

1 Wilma the Witch 9
2 Three Blind Mice 12
3 Bluebird 15
4 Punchinello 19
5 Izzie's Birthday 23
6 Dick Whittington 25
7 London Town 28
8 Giant John 30
9 The Sleeping Beauty 32

Section II: Word Families 37

10 The ZAR 39
11 Mrs. Double EE 42
12 Mr. C. Kay 44
13 The Cross Possum 47
14 The Thareeck 50
15 Rum Dum Dar 52
16 The Little OR 54

Section III: The World Around Us 57

17 Caterpillars and Butterflies 59
18 Floating and Sinking 61
19 Sun and Shadow 63
20 Icarus 66
21 Planet Earth 69
22 Seeds and Fruit 72
23 Seeds and Vegetables 74
24 The Five Senses 76
25 The Five Senses Adventure 79
26 Solids, Liquids, and Gases 82

Section IV: Our Community and Where We Live 85

27 The Doctor 87
28 The Mail Carrier 90
29 The Baker 94
30 The Trash Collector 97
31 Families 99
32 Your Country 102

Section V: Happenings   105

33 The Angry Gnome   107
34 The Ghost from the Past   111
35 Queen Meany   114
36 The Witch Who Wouldn't Wake Up   117

Acknowledgments

The embryo of this book was created some years ago by me and two of my best students ever: Paul Carter and Mary-Ann Lomax. Without our triangular buzz-sessions and in-school trials and tribulations it would never have been written. In spite of the fact that these lessons are now so rewritten as to be perhaps unrecognizable to them, I would like to express here my gratitude to Paul and Mary-Ann for their initial contribution of brains, patience, application, humor, and cooperation. Long live the Class of '76!

I would also like to express my appreciation of the work done by Adria Klein and Donna Bouvier. They have edited this book so cleverly that my American readers can now easily understand it instead of wrinkling their brows over my incomprehensible Australianisms!

Introduction

These days there is a great deal of talk about "back to basics." I believe that drama and play are basic to the skills of reading and writing. But many teachers are reluctant to provide, or are apprehensive about providing, drama classes for their youngest students.

I have written this book to show teachers how children learn through drama and play, and to give people who have never taken a drama lesson before the confidence to teach drama to youngsters.

Confidence is the key. That is why I have chosen to follow a tight, step-by-step format telling you what to do and when. Once the drama lesson is no longer a terrifying unknown, you can simply follow the interests and needs of the children in your class. Until that time, I offer you this book as a prescriptive prop. With confidence, you and your class will put it aside and go it alone!

Children learn through drama and play. They learn to read by reading.[1] They learn to write by writing.[2] And they learn to talk by talking.

Children learn to talk long before they come to school. They are not "taught" by their parents. They learn language because at home:

- they hear language used as a whole,
- they have people to interact with,
- they need to use language for different purposes,[3]
- there are sympathetic adults striving to understand them,
- they are encouraged to learn,
- they live with people who demonstrate the correct form.

So home is a wonderful learning environment. Schools, unfor-

---

[1] Frank Smith quoting Michael Halliday in "The Uses of Language," *Language Arts*, Vol. 54, No. 6, Sept. 1977.

[2] Donald H. Graves, *Writing: Teachers and Children at Work*. Portsmouth, NH: Heinemann, 1983.

[3] Frank Smith (*op. cit.*) has listed the functions of language. Here is my simplified version of that list. We talk in order to ask for things, boss people about, be friendly, reveal who we are through our opinions, find out things we need to know, pretend, and wish and hope with, tell something, crack jokes, lay down rules, and record and reflect on what is past.

tunately, aren't geared to encouraging lots of practice in talking. In the classroom, teachers talk far more often than children do. But if we learn to talk by talking, isn't it children who should be getting the practice in classrooms? Most teachers are well aware that they ought to teach all four elements of language: reading, writing, speaking, and listening. But it is reading and writing that they concentrate on. Listening and speaking are more difficult to structure.

Drama is the perfect vehicle. It provides a ready-made structure for practice in listening and speaking.

How drama can help to develop language

Drama is the one lesson in the curriculum where children have ample opportunities to practice listening and speaking. They can practice language in a context that is real for them, rather than in isolated, teacher-set exercises. In drama lessons, children practice talking by:

- bossing each other around,
- asking questions,
- making suggestions,
- trying to be friendly,
- giving opinions,
- pretending to be other people in role-play,
- demanding things,
- informing other people,
- organizing themselves through problem-solving, and
- reflecting on what happens.

Without this opportunity to play with language, children will grow up to be less articulate than they otherwise might.

How children learn through play

Play is a happy and effective way for children to learn, because:

- it is voluntary,
- it is controlled by the players,
- it sets up challenges the children meet—often with great risk,
- it is fun,
- children can make mistakes without reprimand,
- children are relaxed and, therefore, receptive, and
- children set their own goals.

Drama is like play

Drama is a more directed form of play. It has time limits and limited space, but the essential ingredients are there. If play is a happy and effective way to learn, then drama must be too!

The lessons in this book give you ideas about how and what children can learn through drama.

There are lessons in which children develop their imaginations, organizing abilities, confidence, and language. There are drama-across-the-curriculum lessons in which children learn about the EE word families, or how solids differ from liquids, or where butterflies come from.

But all drama lessons help children learn to read. In learning to read, children need three kinds of knowledge:

1 They need to know how language works (drama gives them opportunities to discover that).
2 They need to know how the wider world organizes itself (drama presents many different situations, stories, and ideas that help to explain that).
3 They need a knowledge of print (which may or may not be part of a drama class).

When does drama fit into the timetable?

Drama should not be scheduled as the last thing on Friday! The value of drama is as a problem-solving exercise. Put drama anywhere it fits: early in the morning, in a social studies lesson, in a lesson on word families, in a lesson on adding and subtracting money. Drama belongs everywhere.

Where should I teach drama?

Drama should never be taught outdoors, unless it's part of a happening. Voices get carried away in the wind. Children get carried away by excitement. Ideally, a large, empty room is where drama works best—where children aren't on top of each other. They need their own space; and space is one of the things I need, to succeed as a drama teacher—unless I'm involved in a happening. Pushing the desks back is all right for an impromptu drama lesson, but it's to be avoided if possible.

What about discipline?

The best teachers of drama tend to be the most experienced teachers in any school. Here are a few hints to keep things under control.

- If the floor of the drama room is slippery (i.e., made of linoleum or polished wood), either make the children keep their shoes and socks on, or make them go barefoot. Socks act like skates: it's thrilling for the kids to slide around, but murder for the teacher.
- Never try to give instructions to a noisy group. But don't wait for total silence—you'll never get it!

3

- Never give instructions at the top of your voice to children scattered around the room. Always draw the children close to you. Give all the instructions necessary for the next activity, and only then allow the children to move away.
- Use a drum, a tambourine, or a gong to attract attention. The human voice can't be heard above a happy, busy drama class.
- With inexperienced children, structure the lesson so that failure is impossible. Activities should be done as a whole class at first, with no individual or group exposure. Activities should not be alien to the child. Pretending to write a story is easier than pretending to walk on a floor covered in honey!
- Don't be thrown by kids who refuse to believe in make-believe. If a child says, "You were the witch, weren't you?" don't say, "Of course I wasn't." Tell the truth. Tell the child that you were, indeed, the witch and then say, "Can't you pretend like the others? They know I was the witch too, but they had good fun pretending that the witch was real. See if you can pretend next time. It's fantastic fun!"

What do children gain from drama?

Apart from the many advantages already stated, I think one of the loveliest advantages of drama is that it gives all children the chance to be successful. A child who fails at reading and math can end up with poor self-esteem because success at school seems so elusive. Drama is essentially about play and talk, and is therefore less threatening to so-called "dumb kids." If children can succeed in drama, the success, the praise, and the respect from their peers will please them so much that their other work will be affected positively.

Another advantage of drama is the group feeling that develops in a class through a closer understanding and knowledge of each other. Instead of the class relating only to the teacher, the children relate to each other and become more tolerant, more settled, and more mature. In my own classes in a college of advanced education, the students who work with me in drama in their very first term remain close friends with the people in that first group because they know each other so well.

What do teachers gain from drama?

Just as children reveal themselves in writing, so they do in drama. The advantage of drama for any teacher is that it gives a completely new perspective on each child. It may show you that a child is popular. It may show that a child who seemed quiet and reserved has in fact got a fantastic sense of humor. It may reveal that a child who is very bright is also a social bully.

I am ashamed to say that I sometimes prejudge a few of my students as "dull," "humorless," "boring," "quiet," "unimaginative," or "unadventurous." Then I either read their writing or see them in a drama improvisation, and I am amazed by how differently they present themselves. I have to rethink my assessment drastically. The value of drama in getting to know your class is absolutely incalculable.

What if I fail?

Of course you will fail—sometimes. We learn only by doing things and making mistakes. Mistakes are important in learning anything, as long as you are controlling the goals and setting up the challenges. We learn to talk by talking. We learn to read by reading. We learn to write by writing. We learn to teach drama by teaching drama. If you do fail, discuss it with the children. Ask them to help you to think about why you failed. Ask them to join you in an experiment to see if you can succeed. See? It's easy!

What you need to know about this book before you begin

This book of drama lessons is arranged in five sections covering song and dance, word families, the world around us, our community, and happenings. Some lessons can be worked up into a little performance for another class or parents. Each lesson is in a step-by-step format of dialogue and directions, which you can follow as closely as you need to.

A list of what you will need is given with each lesson along with a symbol that will give you an idea of how long the lesson runs:

A long lesson that could take several sessions.

About 45 minutes.

About 30 minutes.

Loosely defined age groups ("all," "younger," "older") are provided for each lesson. The categories are deliberately general because you know your class best. Don't feel you should not do a lesson only because it's recommended for children who are older or younger than your group.

Many lessons incorporate stories, or have stories as a classroom follow-up. I have recommended books that I have found fun. You may have your own favorites that fit in with the lesson beautifully.

Music is important. You will need either a tape recorder or a record player. Most schools will have one or the other. Tapes are probably easier to use than records. Your local library may have tapes you can borrow so that you have the music to create the right mood.

It is vital to keep smiling and to be encouraging. That's why I have included lots of praise words, such as "terrific," in the text.

Now it's over to you.

All the best!

Section ▌ Song and Dance

The lessons in this section are full of fun
with songs, action, and stories. There is
a progression in lessons 1 to 4 that will
help children develop an awareness of
what drama is and what is expected of
them. Lesson 9, "The Sleeping Beauty,"
can be worked up into a performance,
with costumes if you like, for parents or
for another class.

1 Wilma the Witch

You will need   A bag of crackers, nuts, etc. hidden in the room before the lesson.

A letter from Wilma the Witch with jam (or jelly) on it.

> Zunday
>
> Dear
>
> I have lozt my zpell book. Pleaze could you help me find it. Juzt do what you did before. (I am Zure the children will help.)
>
> Love from Wilma xxx

Come and sit close to me. Have you ever played the "What Am I?" game? It's really easy. I describe myself and then you see if you can guess what I am. Ready? I'm round. I'm sometimes found on the walls of classrooms. I have a big hand and a little hand and I go "Tick, tock." What am I? You guessed it—a clock. Now who else would like a turn?

Several children take turns. Even if they describe themselves badly, the game still provides a lot of fun because guessing becomes so hard!

May I have another turn? I'm old. I wear black. I have a broomstick and a black pointy hat. What am I? A witch! You guessed easily. Tell me all you know about witches.

Younger

To encourage the children to speak in sentences, avoid questions they can answer with one word such as, "What's a witch's pot called?" (A cauldron.) Instead, ask questions such as, "Who can tell me how witches make their spells?"

9

Find a space where you can turn around without touching anyone or anything. That space is your space, no one else's. You'd better remember exactly where it is, or you'll be in trouble when we start making spells.

As you give the next instructions, demonstrate the actions for the children.

Close your eyes and turn around once to make magic. In front of you there's a big, black witch's hat. Put it on. Now put on the dirty, old, black cape that's at your feet. Be careful not to knock your hat off! Sit down and close your eyes. You're now a really good witch. Your teeth are horribly black and some of them are missing. Your nails are long and dirty. Your back is bent. Your voice is crackly. Open your eyes. You have a broomstick beside you. I'll close my eyes while you hide it in a secret place somewhere in this room. Be sure to come back to your space or else I might guess where your broomstick is. Are you ready? Off you go. Can I open my eyes? Yes. Well done. You don't look as if you moved at all.
Creep over to me, all you witches. We are going to make spells. I'm going to put rotten leaves and moldy jam sandwiches and dead dogs' eyes in my cauldron. What are you going to put in yours?

As the children reply, the more imaginative ones will give the others ideas for really revolting ingredients, so that when they make their spells, the children will all know what to do.

Right. Back to your spaces. Show me where your cauldron is by putting your horrible hands around it. To make your spell you have to say out loud everything that you put in. And don't forget where your cauldron is—we don't want the spells to get mixed up, do we? Off you go!

Allow time for the children to make their spells. Wander about, chatting to the witches and helping anyone who needs it.

While you stir your nasty spell you should chant these words in a ghastly crackly voice:

> *Round and round the cauldron go,*
> *Now stir fast,*
> *Now stir slow.*

You may need to practice the chant once or twice with the children.

Now, while I hide my eyes, find your broomstick, wave it over your cauldron to make it disappear, then throw the broomstick in the air and say "Wheee!" Off you go. I promise not to look.
Now your spell will really work. Come over here, everyone. Guess what? I have a friend who is a witch. Her name is

Wilma. As I was leaving home this morning, I found a letter on my doormat. I know it's from Wilma because it's very messy. Look at this. It's jam. She must have written the letter at break-fast. Smell the jam. Now what does Wilma say? Would someone like to read it to the rest of us?

Give Wilma's letter to a child to read. Talk about the funny mistakes that Wilma makes.

Well, I know what that means! We can only help her if there are at least ten children here. Are there? Who'll count for us?

One child counts. Then all count again together for luck!

Now all of you have to be under nine years old. Are you? No tens? No elevens? Any ones? Heh heh . . . Next, we need to be able to come up with five words that rhyme with witch. Can you think of any?

Rich, ditch, pitch, hitch, stitch, twitch.

Last of all we have to sing the ABC song. Ready?

All sing the alphabet song to the tune of "Twinkle, twinkle, little star."

> *A, B, C, D, E, F, G,*
> *H, I, J, K, L, M, N, O, P,*
> *Q, R, S,*
> *T, U, V,*
> *W, X, Y, and Z.*
> *Now I've sung my A-B-C's.*
> *Next time won't you sing with me?*

(Whisper:)

If we have helped Wilma find her spell book, she may have hidden a nice surprise for us to say thank you. Let's see if she has.

Of course someone finds the little bag of goodies that you hid so carefully before the lesson began!

Oh, great! She came! As you go you can each have one. They're magic and they'll make you good for the rest of the day.

2 Three Blind Mice

You will need   A pink hat—Wilma's special hat.

Stories

The Church Mice at Bay by Graham Oakley. New York: Atheneum, 1979.

The Church Mouse by Graham Oakley. New York: Atheneum, 1972.

Poems

"Mice" by Rose Fyleman. From *The Faber Book of Nursery Verse*, edited by Barbara Ireson. Winchester, MA: Faber & Faber, 1982.

"The Mouse" by Elizabeth Coatsworth. From *Rainbow in the Sky*, collected and edited by Louis Untermeyer. San Diego, CA: Harcourt Brace Jovanovich, 1985.

Music

Music to mime being a mouse to; you could use a xylophone.

Do you remember how you helped Wilma before? What did you do to help her find her spell book? Will you help her again? You see, Wilma is taking a vacation on a farm, and she's in trouble because her cat won't stop chasing the three blind mice that belong to the farmer's wife. Wilma has left me her special mouse-chasing spell hat, which is why it's a pink hat instead of a witch's hat. Isn't it revolting? If you're as quiet as mice when I have Wilma's hat on, the cat won't chase the mice. So watch the hat carefully. When it's on, you have to be quiet and still.

Let's practice the hat trick while we sing "Three Blind Mice." I am going to see if I can trick you.

Sing "Three Blind Mice" all together. Keep putting the hat on and taking it off.

I have a little mouse in my hand.

Younger

(Mime it.)

Ooh, it's sweet! Its feet are tickling my palm. You hold a mouse in your hand, too. Stroke its fur. What's your mouse doing? And yours? Mine's white. What color is yours?

I have some cheese. I'm going to feed my mouse now. Ooh, look. He loves it. You feed your mouse, too.

Read the class a story or a poem about mice. I love the poem "Mice" by Rose Fyleman and the story *The Church Mice at Bay* by Graham Oakley, with the picture of the vicar naked in front of the Worplethorpe procession. Children laugh a lot at that illustration!

Somewhere in this room is your mouse's cage.

Point to where it is.

Now very gently put your mouse back in its cage.

Can you remember your very own space? Go to that space and lie down in it. Can you curl up smaller than that? Marvelous. Now you're a mouse. You have little claws, thin legs,

white fur, pink eyes, twitchy whiskers and a long tail. What will you do when you wake up? Will you clean yourself? Or eat some cheese? Or explore your cage? When you hear the music, wake up and be a mouse. Off you go!

Play mouse music (or the xylophone). Let the children be mice for as long as they seem able to concentrate. It takes a while for a person to "grow" into being a mouse!

And now the mouse is going to sleep again in its own little space, all curled up and snug.

Now, as quietly as mice, make a big circle. Let's sing "Three Blind Mice," clapping to the beat as we do it. Lovely! Now, we'll sing it with some movement.

Three blind mice,	Hands over eyes. Three steps into the middle.
Three blind mice,	Three steps back.
See how they run,	Turn around.
See how they run!	Turn around the other way.
They all ran after the farmer's wife,	Run around in a big circle.
Who cut off their tails with a carving knife,	Scissors action with arms.
Did you ever see such a thing in your life	Turn round once, hands circling eyes.
As three blind mice?	Three big claps.

Repeat as often as you think fit.

Just before we go back to class, could you get your mouse out of its cage and then come and sit by me. Think of a word—any word—that rhymes with mice. Now line up at the door and whisper your word to me. And don't squash your mouse! We'll put it into a big cage with all the other mice in the classroom.

3 Bluebird

You will need The pink hat from the previous lesson.

A letter from Wilma—keep it messy.

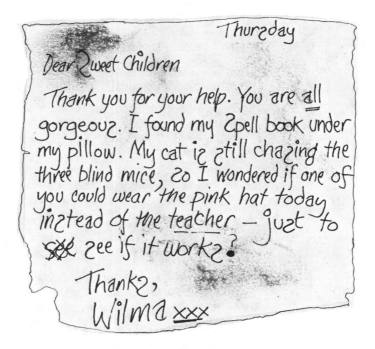

Thursday

Dear Sweet Children

Thank you for your help. You are all gorgeous. I found my spell book under my pillow. My cat is still chasing the three blind mice, so I wondered if one of you could wear the pink hat today instead of the teacher — just to see see if it works?

Thanks,
Wilma xxx

Stories

The Dead Bird by Margaret Wise Brown. New York: Young Scott, 1965.

The Happy Prince by Oscar Wilde. New York: Oxford University Press, 1980.

Are You My Mother? by P. D. Steadman. New York: Random House, 1960.

Lifetimes by Bryan Mellonie and Robert Ingpen. New York: Bantam Books, 1983.

Have You Seen Birds? by Joanne Oppenheim. Richmond Hill, Ontario: Scholastic-TAB Publications, 1986.

Younger

Music

Music for miming birds flying, such as a xylophone or "The Hall of the Mountain King" from *Peer Gynt* by Edvard Grieg.

Remember Wilma? Well, I found this letter on my desk yesterday afternoon. Would you like to read it? Who would like to try?

Ask a child to read the letter, if possible.

Now choose someone to play the pink hat trick and remind the children to be still and quiet when the hat is on. Place the pink hat on your lap for the next game.

Let's play "Who am I?"

I'm dressed in red. I have a long beard. I live at the North Pole, and I receive lots of letters at Christmas. Who am I? Santa Claus, of course!

Allow three or four children to have a turn.

May I have another turn, please? I'm big and I'm yellow and I have feathers and two legs and you see me on television. Big Bird! That's right! What do you know about birds? Anything. Tell me.

Right, off you go to your very own space. Close your eyes and turn round once for magic. When you open your eyes you'll be a bird. When the music starts, swoop and fly around the sky, but look out for the pink hat. If you see it on, you must stop still.

Give one child the pink hat and encourage her/him to try to trick the others by putting on the hat in mid-flight, so to speak!

Fly back to your space and perch on your nest. I bet some of you were eagles, and I think I saw a magpie. Can you think of any other birds that might be flying around today?

Talk about big birds and little birds. Give another bird/child the pink hat and warn the others.

This time, let's see if there's a big difference between one bird and another. What sort of bird will you be? When the music starts, fly around until I say, "Stop." Off you go, birds! . . .

Stop!

There were lots of different birds. Come and sit by me. We're going to learn a song about a bluebird. We can do a dance to it too. Let's make a circle and drop hands. You sing the song and I'll be the bluebird.

Learn the bluebird song and actions.

Here comes a blue-bird thru my win-dow,

Here comes a blue-bird thru my door. Here comes a blue-bird

thru my win-dow, Hey did-dle dump-ty dee.

Have a lit-tle hop and a skip in the cor-ner,

Have a lit-tle hop and a skip with me. Have a lit-tle hop and a

skip in the cor-ner, Hey did-dle dump-ty dee.

Here comes a Bluebird thru my window
Here comes a Bluebird thru my door.
Here comes a Bluebird thru my window
Hey diddle dumpty dee.

Children sing while the bluebird weaves in and out between them.

17

*Have a little hop and a skip in
the corner.
Have a little hop and a skip with
me.
Have a little hop and a skip in
the corner.
Hey diddle dumpty dee.*

Children clap and sing;
the bluebird chooses a
partner and dances.

Part with a bow.
The partner becomes the
new bluebird.

*I'm too old to be a bluebird! I should have been an ostrich
instead. Who'd like a turn? What bird will you be? A hawk?
Terrific.*

Here comes a magpie through my window, etc.

Allow as many children as possible to have a turn without
their interest fading. Read the children the story you have chosen. Warn them if it is going to be sad.

*Can you all lie on the floor as still as a dead bird? Almost
without breathing? Aaah, you're so clever! Even your eyes
aren't moving. Well done. I really should bury you properly,
but if I did, you wouldn't be able to eat your lunch (or whatever meal is next)! So you'd better come to life again and we'll
all go and peck at our birdseed. Off we go, flying through the air.
Watch out for that airplane!*

4 Punchinello

You will need A glove puppet.

Music

Sad and happy music, such as Vivaldi's *Four Seasons* and Saint-Saens' *Carnival of the Animals*.

One of Wilma's best friends is a puppet called Punchinello. He's a string puppet. Can anyone tell me how a string puppet works? That's right! Strings are attached to different parts of the puppet (such as its legs and arms and head) so that the person who works the puppet can move all the bits separately. Like this.

Demonstrate simple movements of head, wrists, arms.

I have two different kinds of music here today. I'll play both tapes and then see if you can tell me which is the sad piece and which is the happy piece. Listen to them both.

O.K. Find your very own space and get ready to be Punchinello. You're going to dance a puppet dance. Will it be a sad dance or a happy dance? You'll know when you hear the music. Off you go!

Play sad music.

Oh, wonderful, I can tell a mile away that you are sad string puppets. Now try the happy dance.

Play happy music.

Great. Come and sit near me. I wonder what makes puppets happy or sad? What makes you happy?

Ask a few children to talk about being happy.

What makes you sad?

Ask a few children to talk about being sad.

I have a puppet here. She's not a string puppet. She's a glove puppet. She's called Dizzie. Would you like to say hello to her? Hello, Dizzie!

Younger

The puppet replies to all the following questions, of course!

Would you like to ask her what makes her happy?

Ask one of the children. A conversation ensues between puppet and children about what makes people sad or happy. Puppet asks open-ended questions such as: "When did you last feel happy?" "What would make you cry?" "What do you like doing best on the weekend?" After a while encourage the children to ask the puppet questions—where she lives and works, what she eats, who her family is, etc.

(Puppet says)

I know a song and dance that will make us all really happy. It goes like this.

Teach the children the song and then the actions.

MUSIC ARRANGED BY LESLEY COX

Ah, who comes here, Punch-i-nel-lo, lit-tle fel-low?

Ah, who comes here, Punch - i - nel - lo, lit - tle dear?

What can you do, Punch-i- nel-lo, lit-tle fel - low?

What can you do, Punch - i - nel - lo, lit - tle dear?

We'll do it too, Punch-i-nel-lo, lit-tle fel-low.

We'll do it too, Punch - i - nel - lo, lit - tle dear.

Ah, who comes here,
Punchinello, little fellow?
Ah, who comes here,
Punchinello, little dear?
What can you do, Punchinello,
little fellow?
What can you do, Punchinello,
little dear?
We'll do it, too, Punchinello,
little fellow
We'll do it, too, Punchinello,
little dear.

Teacher (as Punchinello)
stands out front and
thinks of an action.

Children imitate Punchi-
nello.
Teacher/Punchinello
chooses the next person to
be out front.

Come and sit by me. What's a word that rhymes with puppet? Muppet! Clever you. What's a Muppet?

Let the children tell you about their favorite Muppet.

And a word that rhymes with happy? Isn't it hard? Well, I think Punchinello was a happy chappy, don't you? Last time I taught this lesson we found three words to rhyme with sad! I wonder if you can beat that record? Bad. Yes! Had, mad, dad, lad. Five! You're brilliant.

5 Izzie's Birthday

You will need

Story

The Surprise Party by Pat Hutchins. New York: Penguin/Puffin Books, 1972.

Sit around me. I have a friend called Izzie the elf. She's so small she can sit on my hand. I like her because one day when I'd forgotten my lunch, she helped me to remember it, so I turned my car around and went home again to get it. She's really kind.

I got this from her this morning.

Mime taking an invitation out of your bag.

This is an invitation to me, and to all of you, too, to her birthday party. She says you've all got your own invitation. You're sitting on it. Is she right? Yes! Look. Hold up yours.

All mimed, naturally.

Throw the envelopes into this basket.

Walk round with real wastepaper basket for mimed envelopes to be thrown into.

I'll read my invitation to you. Can you tell me what your invitation says?

Let several children tell you what their invitation says.

Will you come with me to Elf World? Yes? All right then, put your head on your knees and cross your fingers while I say this rhyme.

> *Hocus pocus rattle tum tee*
> *Hold on tight, and come with me!*
> *Hocus pocus rattle tum tar*
> *Open your eyes, 'cos here we are!*

Oh, isn't Izzie kind! Look—we've all got presents. You see, elves give presents on their birthdays, they don't get presents. Can I open mine first? Perfume! I love it. Would you like to smell it?

Let them have a sniff.

Isn't it lovely? Now you open yours. Tell each other what you have. Describe its size and color and how it works or what it does.

All

23

Leave time for everyone to describe their presents.

Put all your paper and ribbon in the wastepaper basket.

Real basket again—mimed paper wrappings.

Now put your presents carefully at the edge of the room. Well! Now look what we've got! A birthday cake each. With candles, too. Let's all sing Izzie a Happy Birthday song.

All sing.

Now let's all blow out the candles. WHOOOO!
Let's each cut a piece of cake and eat it. Careful with the knife; show it to me. Cut your cake and eat a piece. Ooh, mine's chocolate with whipped cream in the middle. What have you got? And you? Can I have a bite? Yum!
She's given us a balloon too. Blow it up. Blow. Blow. Blow. Now tie a knot in it. Play with your balloon around the room.

Play the game "K-I-N-G spells king" (also known as "Red Light"), but use the phrase "I-Z-Z-I-E spells Izzie": One child stands at one end of the classroom, facing the wall. The rest of the class stands at the other end of the room. When the first child begins to say, "I-Z-Z-I-E spells Izzie," the other children move as far forward as they can before the first child turns around. The aim is to touch the wall before the speaker turns around. If the speaker sees anyone move when he or she turns around, the person seen has to go back to the other end of the room again. The child who is doing the talking may speak slowly or quickly or both, but can turn around only when he or she has finished saying the sentence "I-Z-Z-I-E spells Izzie." If any child reaches, say, halfway, that child must freeze when the speaker turns around, to avoid being sent back. When the speaker begins to spell again, the children creep further forward, until one child eventually reaches the wall. That child then becomes the speaker.

Let's all write a thank-you letter to Izzie.

Mime finding paper and pencil and writing the letter.

It's time to go. Close your eyes, heads on knees, fingers crossed.

> *Hocus pocus rattle tum tee,*
> *Close your eyes and fly with me!*
> *Hocus pocus rattle tum tome*
> *Open your eyes 'cos we're at home!*

Give me your letters to Izzie and I'll mail them. Thank you. Thanks. Thank you . . .
Now come and sit by me. I'm going to read you a story about a party.

Read *The Surprise Party* by Pat Hutchins.

6 Dick Whittington

You will need   The story of Dick Whittington, such as:

Dick Whittington, edited by Vera Southgate. Bedford Hills, NY: Merry Thoughts.

Dick Whittington as told by Catherine Storr. Milwaukee, WI: Raintree Publishers, 1985.

Sit down here and watch me walk. I'm going to walk in two different ways—once as a king and once as a poor, tired, hungry boy. Which one am I doing now?

   Walk like a poor boy.

   And now?

   Walk like a poor boy again!

   And now?

All   Walk like a king.

*Let's all be kings. We're going to inspect our soldiers. My sol-
diers are standing in a line here. Where are yours? Off we go,
straight backs, chins up, stern faces.*

*Now let's be the poor boy. Would he be happy or sad if he
were hungry? Let's have really sad faces as we walk along the
road towards London. Terrific! Come and sit by me.*

Ask the children if anyone knows where London is. Tell,
rather than read, the story of Dick Whittington and include the
children. For example, when Dick sleeps on the doorstep of
Fitzgerald's house, the children sleep. Wake them up by being
the cook yelling at Dick to go away. When Dick buys his cat,
the children hold up two pennies, one in each hand. Children
stroke their cats while you finish the story.

*Now let's all be Dick. As I sing the song, wherever you are,
you turn and walk in another direction. Find your own space.
Now start walking when I sing.*

> *Turn again, Whittington,*
> *Lord Mayor of London Town.*
> *Turn again, Whittington,*
> *Thrice Mayor of London Town.*
> *Turn again, Whittington,*
> *Lord Mayor of London Town.*

Keep going until the children become bored. The song is easy,
with a beat like church bells. You could say it if you wanted to,
or if you don't know the tune.

*Who knows another song about London Town? "London
Bridge is Falling Down"? Terrific. Let's sing it:*

> *London Bridge is falling down,*
> *Falling down, falling down.*
> *London Bridge is falling down,*
> *My fair lady.*

> *We can build it up again,*
> *Up again, up again.*
> *We can build it up again,*
> *My fair lady.*

> *Now it's standing strong and tall,*
> *Strong and tall, strong and tall.*
> *Now it's standing strong and tall,*
> *My fair lady.*

Now let's stand in two straight lines facing each other. Look at
the person opposite you and hold your arms high with just fin-
gertips touching so that all together we make the bridge. What a
wonderful bridge! Now, as we sing, we're going to fall to the floor
very slowly.Then we're going to be builders with bricks and

*wood and nails and hammers. We're going to build the bridge
as we sing the second verse, and in the last verse we'll stand
like a tall bridge again. Ready?*

Sing "London Bridge" again with all the actions.

Terrific! Let's all walk like kings and queens!

7 London Town

You will need Another messy letter from Wilma saying how wonderful the children are and how much she enjoyed the lesson about her friend Punchinello.

I have the most terrible memory! I can hardly remember the story of Dick Whittington. Can you? What happened first?

Elicit the story from the children.

I think we should all go to London today, but:

> *Which is the way to London Town,*
> *To see the king in his golden crown?*
> *Left, right, up and down,*
> *That's the way to London Town.*

> *Which is the way to London Town,*
> *To see the queen in her velvet gown?*
> *One foot up and one foot down,*
> *That's the way to London Town.*

Can you say that with me?

All say it together.

Let's walk this time, up to the other end of the room.

Walk up on the first verse and back on the other.

Terrific. This time I'll ask you the way to London Town as we walk and you all tell me the answer.

You say the first two lines, children say the last two, in both verses.

Off we go!
Who else went to London to look at the queen? Does anyone know? The pussycat! Of course. Who can say the rhyme for us?

Choose all the children who think they can recite it, ask them to stand together and say the poem to the others.

> *Pussycat, pussycat,*
> *Where have you been?*

> *I've been to London*
> *To look at the queen.*

All

Pussycat, pussycat,
What did you there?

I frightened a little mouse
Under her chair.

Let's all say it together. Now you are the pussycat and answer my questions.

You say the first two lines then the children answer with the next two lines.

Hey, I heard some awful news! Guess what?

London's burning!
London's burning!

Call the engines!
Call the engines!

Fire! Fire!
Fire! Fire!

Pour on water!
Pour on water!

Let's all sing it!

Now let's do some great actions to it, in each corner of the room. We'll start in this corner and sing it through here, with actions. After that we'll move to the next corner.

Stand with the children in one corner and demonstrate the actions as you sing the song.

London's burning! *London's burning!*	Hands over face shocked.
Call the engines! *Call the engines!*	Make big beckoning gestures.
Fire! Fire! *Fire! Fire!*	Hands cupped around mouth.
Pour on water! *Pour on water!*	Pouring action.

Once the song plus actions have been mastered, you and the children can move from corner to corner—a new corner for each action. Discipline must be as tight as possible.

Whew! Thank you! We've saved London from burning.

You've worked very hard! Let's go back to the classroom and have a rest. Perhaps there'll be a letter from Wilma.

There is, of course.

8 Giant John

You will need

Stories

"The Brave Little Tailor" from *Grimm's Fairy Tales*, tr. by Peter Carter. New York: Oxford University Press, 1982.

The Brave Little Tailor, retold by Robert D. San Souci. New York: Doubleday, 1982.

Giant Tales, Corrine Denan. Mahwah, NJ: Troll Associates.

Jack and the Beanstalk, edited by Vera Southgate. Bedford Hills, NY: Merry Thoughts.

Music

Music to be a giant to, such as "The Grande Finale" from *Carnival of the Animals* by Saint-Saens.

Tell the children the story of the Brave Little Tailor who killed seven at one blow.

Find your very own space. You're going to be giants. Giants walk with big steps and they have big voices. Whenever you meet a giant you'll shake hands and say, "Hello! I'm a giant! Who are you?" and the other person will say, "I'm a giant too!" Off we go, walking around a giant town. "Hello! I'm a giant" Who are you?" etc.
Terrific! Now listen to this music.

Play a short excerpt from "The Grande Finale" in Saint-Saens' *Carnival of the Animals*.

Who might move to music like that? A giant? No! Who then? A mouse? Yes! A butterfly? A fly? Yes. A fairy? Yes. I'll play it again and you can be a fairy (or a goblin) cleaning your house in a terrific hurry. Off you go!
That was wonderful. Sit by me. I have a song here about giants and fairies. I'll sing it, and then we'll all sing it together.

Sing the song to the tune of "Skip to My Lou."

All

Giant John is big and strong,
Giant John is big and strong,
Giant John is big and strong,
Move like a giant slowly.

Little fairies are small and light (etc.),
Fly like a fairy quickly.

Let us guess what you are (etc.),
A fairy or a giant moving.

We can have actions with this song. Stand in a circle and walk
around slowly for Giant John. Run around with little steps for
the fairy. Then for the third verse we'll have one person in the
middle being an angry giant or a busy fairy. We'll have to guess
which it is. Off we go!

Repeat the entire song each time. The child in the middle re-
joins the circle but chooses someone else to be in the middle
for the third verse. Keep going for as long as the children seem
to be enjoying the song.

Super! Now it's time for class. I want to read you a story
about giants to finish the lesson.

9 The Sleeping Beauty

You will need   Gummed stars.

Stories

The story of Sleeping Beauty. There are many versions. We include the traditional version and a beautifully illustrated edition.

"Briar Rose." From *Grimm's Fairy Tales*, tr. by Peter Carter. New York: Oxford University Press, 1982.

Thorn Rose, illustrated by Errol Le Cain. New York: Penguin/Puffin Books, 1978.

Sleeping Beauty and Other Favourite Fairy Tales, tr. by Angela Carter. New York: Shocken Books, 1984.

Sleeping Beauty, retold by Mercer Mayer. New York: Macmillan, 1984.

This lesson works towards a performance—for parents or for another class. The music and actions are as old as the hills. I can remember being the princess at school in 1952! Old or not, it works! If you had an entire day you could learn it all in that time. The lessons are written out without an obvious break; it's up to you to stop and start to fit in with your timetable.

Tell the story of Sleeping Beauty. Show the pictures afterwards.

Who knows what a graduation is? There is usually a big party at a graduation. When I have a party I clean my house really well and I make lots of different things to eat. I wish I had maids to do the cleaning and a cook to do the cooking and a gardener to make the garden tidy. Kings and queens are really lucky—they have lots of maids and cooks and gardeners.

Tell me what a maid might do to make the castle ready for a big party.

If you were a cook, what would you bake for a party?

Can you imagine how big the gardens would be around a castle? What might the gardener have to do?

What do you think the wicked fairy would do to get ready for a graduation that she hadn't been invited to?

Find your very own space. Are you going to be a maid, a cook, a gardener, or a wicked fairy getting ready for the graduation? I'll walk around and see if I can guess who you are and

The Rehearsal

The Performance

All

32

what you're doing. I'll play some music while we work. Off you go!

Play music as background—it tends to make the silence of mime less inhibiting.

Terrific! Come and tell the class who you were and what you were doing.

Choose five or six children to explain their characters and actions. Give each child a gummed star.

This star is a magic star. Stick it on your forehead and you will sleep for a hundred years or until you get a kiss to wake you up. Lie down comfortably. Close your eyes.

Sing the children the Sleeping Beauty song. Wake them up with a kiss on each child's hand.

Let's all be that wicked witch. I know you can make terrific spells already, just like Wilma. Find your space, you mean old things, and make the most horrible spell you can think of. Oooh, yuk! Great! You make me feel sick.
Now then—how about we all learn the song?

Sing each verse once alone, then again with the children.

Oh, once there was a princess, *A princess, a princess,* *Oh, once there was a princess,* *Long, long ago.*	Princess sits sewing or reading. All others point to her.
She lived up in a tower high, *A tower high, a tower high,* *She lived up in a tower high,* *Long, long ago.*	Children make a tower with arms raised.

The wicked witch she cast her
   spell,
Cast her spell, cast her spell,
The wicked witch she cast her
   spell,
Long, long ago.
	Witch moves downstage to cast her spell.
	
	Witch moves back to her place.

The princess slept for a hundred
   years,
A hundred years, a hundred
   years,
The princess slept for a hundred
   years,
Long, long ago.
	All children pretend to sleep, heads on hands.

A thorny hedge grew all around, *All around, all around,* *A thorny hedge grew all around,* *Long, long ago.*	Thorny hedge moves to make a ragged circle around the princess.

A handsome prince came riding by,
Riding by, riding by,
A handsome prince came riding by,
Long, long ago.

Prince moves across the stage and rides around the thorny hedge.

He cut his way through the thorny hedge,
Thorny hedge, thorny hedge,
He cut his way through the thorny hedge,
Long, long ago.

Prince cuts through the hedge. The thorny hedge collapses.

He put her on his big white horse,
Big white horse, big white horse,
He put her on his big white horse
Long, long ago.

Kisses her hand and puts her on horse slowly.

They both rode off on their big white horse,
Big white horse, big white horse,
They both rode off on their big white horse,
Long, long ago.

Prince and princess ride away through audience.

Children stand, bow to audience and walk off.

MUSIC ARRANGED BY LESLEY COX

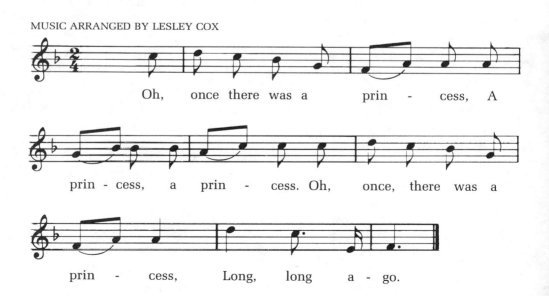

Oh, once there was a prin - cess, A prin - cess, a prin - cess. Oh, once, there was a prin - cess, Long, long a - go.

We need some cooks and maids and gardeners—who'll be those? Who'd like to be the thorny hedge? And the prince? And the witch? And the princess? Splendid.

In a group of 32 there might be 16 maids, cooks, gardeners; 13 for the thorny hedge; and a prince, a princess, and a wicked witch. If you have problems with casting, choose the princess and then write all the other parts on cards and put them in a hat which the children can lucky-dip into.

Only you know how many rehearsals you will need. When you're ready, perform the play to an audience. It gives the children a great feeling of achievement and importance. If it is a special occasion the children may like to dress up.

Have fun!

The stage is best set up like this:

xxxxxxxxxxxxxxxxx singers
xxxxxxxxxxxxx thorny hedge

x witch   x prince

o
Princess on a stool

Audience

Section II  Word Families

Children greatly enjoy these lessons
about sounds and word families. They
are suitable for children who already
have an understanding of the reading
process and will therefore appreciate the
fun and be able to participate fully in
the drama and games with Mrs. Double
EE and Mr. C. Kay, etc.

10 The ZAR

The AR word family

You will need An alphabet necklace. Write each letter of the alphabet on a card. Use a string to make each card into a necklace that will easily slip over the children's heads. You may need an extra T and S.

Music

Music for being an elephant to, such as "The Elephant" from *Carnival of the Animals* by Saint-Saens.

Lay the alphabet necklaces out in order in two lines on the floor, A to L, M to Z.

Sit down close to me. That's the alphabet lying on the floor so let's sing the alphabet song!

A, B, C, D, E, F, G,
H, I, J, K, L, M, N, O, P,
Q, R, S,
T, U, V,
W, X, Y, Z.
Now I've sung my A-B-C's.
Next time won't you sing with me?

Ask a child to find the letter A, put it on, and stand facing the class. Ask another child to pick out the letter R and stand close to A.

Now can you tell me what sound it makes? AR! "Ahr." Excellent!
Can you think of any words with AR in them that make an "ahr" sound? Tar, car, bar, far, jar, *etc.*
What else do we need to make the word car?

Choose a child who answers correctly and allow him/her to put on the C and stand up in the right place.

How could we make cart?

Repeat the operation.

Older

And carts? Terrific!

*C, T, and S can sit down now. Let's make another word.
Which one shall we have?*

Play it by ear and go on for as long as the children find it fun.
Have an extra T and S for *start, stars, tarts,* etc.

Now I'd like to make a word.

Put on the Z and stand beside the AR.

What word is this? I've never heard of a ZAR, have you?
*What might a ZAR look like? What does it eat? Where does it
live? What would it be like? Friendly? Silly? Mean?*

All sit down and discuss the possibilities.

*Let's all be a ZAR. Find your own space and lie down. Close
your eyes and think about being a ZAR. How many legs have
you got? What's your skin like? How big are you? Are you
frightening? Are you shy? When you move, do you walk or roll
or jump or crawl or slither or what? Are there boy ZARs and
girl ZARs?*
*When I play the music, you're going to be a ZAR looking for
food. Off you go!*

Play "The Elephant" from Saint-Saens' *Carnival of the Animals.*

*Super! Find a partner and tell each other all about being a
ZAR.*
Sit round me.
*ZARs just love AR words. They eat AR things. Are cookies an
AR thing? No! Is a tart an AR thing? Yes! Does a ZAR ride a
bike or drive a car? What does he or she prefer—the smell of
perfume or the smell of tar? Which does he or she like best out
of the sun, moon, and stars?*

You should be able to think of many more.

Wow! You're clever!
I have a ZAR song here. I'll sing it first, then we'll all sing it.

Sing the song once to the tune of "Polly Wolly Doodle." Then
sing it, line by line, with the children. Then all sing together.

> *I know a ZAR*
> *Who has a car*
> *Which it drives on the tar all day.*
> *It drives to the farm*
> *Where it waves around its arm,*
> *Then goes to the bars to play.*
> *Well, the ZAR*
> *And its car*

Are driving far today!
It's going to play darts,
And eat jam tarts,
With a friend who lives far away!

How would your ZAR dance? Mine dances like this.

Do something ridiculous.

Let's find our spaces and dance a ZAR dance while we sing the song. Off we go! Super!
I'd love to know what your ZAR looks like. Let's go and paint it.

11 Mrs. Double EE

The EE word family

You will need

A camera —a Polaroid camera, if possible.

Dress-up clothes such as shoes, hat, shawl, glasses, etc.

A blackboard and chalk.

Come and sit by me.

If you have a real camera, great! If you have a Polaroid, even better. Otherwise, mime taking pictures. I always mime it.

I want to take a photo of you. Say "cheese." Lovely! Thanks. Turn to someone near you and say "ee" quietly while I take a few more photos. This is what you were saying: "EE."

Write EE on the board.

EE from the double EE family. Oh, excuse me. I think there's someone outside. I won't be a minute.

Exit and rapidly dress up in old hat, shawl, shoes, and glasses. Re-enter as Mrs. Double EE.

Hello, everyone! My name's Mrs. Double EE. I don't often come to your world, but there were so many lovely EE sounds coming from this room that I thought you might like to come with me to my land: the land of Eeky Peeky. Would you? I'll look after you.
One important thing before we go: whenever you hear a double EE word in Eeky Peeky land, you must say it three times very quickly; otherwise, I'll disappear. Let's practice that. What are some double EE words?

Children suggest some.

I'll say one—tree! Tree! Tree! Tree! Whew! Thank goodness for that. Off we go.
Stay close to me. Close your eyes tight while I say the spell.

All

Iminy, Piminy, one, two, three,
Take me to the land of double EE!
Over the moon and over a star,
Eeky Peeky, here we are.

Open your eyes. I have lots of things to show you, but do re-member what I told you about double EE words, won't you? Right! First we'd better jump over this creek. (Creek! Creek! Creek!) All jump. Good. I hope that you didn't get wet. Would you like to look at my queen? (Queen! Queen! Queen!) Be very quiet. Let's creep (Creep! Creep! Creep!) along this road. Now look through the trees. (Trees! Trees! Trees!) There she is.

Discuss the queen with the class.

Come on. We don't want her to see (See! See! See!) us peep-ing. (Peeping! Peeping! Peeping!)

Let's sit down and have a rest. Guess what we like to eat here? It must have a double EE in it. Ham sandwiches? No. Cheese? (Cheese! Cheese! Cheese!) Yes, of course.

And beets. (Beets! Beets! Beets!) Do you know what you can find swimming in the rivers here? Fish? No. Frogs? No. Eels? (Eels! Eels! Eels!) Yes.

Come along. Let's continue our walk. It's autumn now and the leaves are all over the street. (Street! Street! Street!) We'll have to find a broom and sweep them up. (Sweep! Sweep! Sweep!) Thank you, everyone. We can put the brooms away.

If you feel like more, Mrs. Double EE and the children can:

- walk up a steep hill
- see a swarm of bees,
- hide under a sheet for protection,
- go to the corner shop and buy some sweets—but you may not need money because they are free!

Now, after all those adventures it is time to go to sleep. (Sleep! Sleep! Sleep!)

> *Iminy, Piminy, one two, three,*
> *Take us away from the land of double EE*
> *Over the stars and over the moon*
> *Goodbye, Eeky Peeky, we'll be back soon.*

Open your eyes. Sssh! I think there's someone outside.

Exit and return as yourself.

Hello children! Sorry I've been away from you for a while. What have you been doing? Anything exciting?

Make out that you have no idea about what they've done. Ask questions. Be enthralled. Be puzzled. As they say EE words, write them on the board. Of course the children know it was you, but they suspend disbelief in a most charming manner!

I think Mrs. Double EE was really kind to take you on that trip. Let's write her a special thank-you letter in class.

12 Mr. C. Kay

The CK word family

You will need A letter to the children written in big letters on a large piece of card.

Dear Children,

This is just a qui__ letter. I want to tri__ you by not finishing off some of the words. If you can guess the missing letters you can play an exciting game.

I hope you don't think that this is a si__ joke. The clo__ is ti__ing away. My friend Di__ Whittington wants me to play with him so I must go qui__ly.

Good lu__!

Yours sincerely

C. Kay

Older

44

10 envelopes

Each envelope will contain one of the following instructions sealed inside:

- You are a mother. Pretend that you are spanking a naughty baby over your knee.
- Waddle like a duck.
- Show us how you would look if you were feeling sick.
- Pick some flowers and put them in a vase.
- Put on your shoes and socks.
- Walk backwards.
- Scratch your neck.
- Pretend you are licking an ice cream cone.
- Pretend that you have a ball. Kick it.
- Suck your thumb.

Show the letter to the children.

Can you read this letter? Let's try. Terrific. Does anyone know what letters are missing? K. Yes! Anything else? C. Fantastic! Who'd like to write in the missing letters in "quick"? As you do it, say the word that you're completing.

Ask eight different children until the letter is complete.

Ah good! Now it's easy to read so let's all read it again, together.

I'm sure you'll be able to play Mr. C. Kay's game. Let's practice all together. Do you see the envelopes in this hat? You pick one out, open it, and see what it says. Whoever chooses the envelope has to read the instructions and do what it says. The rest of us have to guess what he or she is doing. If it says, "Waddle like a duck," that's what you would have to do. The first person to find the CK word chooses the next envelope. What's the CK word in "Waddle like a duck"? Like? No! Duck? Yes! The person who was the duck then writes "duck" on the board for us. Let's begin.

Choose someone to begin.

Pick an envelope. Can you read it? I'll help you if you can't. Right! Now do what it says.

And so on until all the envelopes have been opened.

Here's a great poem, called "Popsicles." It has lots of CK words in it.

Lickety, lickety, lickety, lick,
I like Popsicles on a stick.
Cold and tingly on my tongue,
Melting in the bright hot sun.

Drippety, drippety, drippety, drip.
A drop is dribbling from my lip.
Cold drips run down my hand,
Sticking fingers where they land.

Stickety, stickety, stickety, stick.
Ice melts fast, so eat it quick.
Licking Popsicles is such fun—
I think I'll have another one.

Who can tell me just one word from that great poem that has a CK in it. Lickety. Terrific!

Find your very own space. You are a Popsicle, really cold, frozen stiff. When I say "melt," the sun is going to come out and you're going to melt quite slowly until you're just a little dribble on the floor. Are you ready? "Melt!"

You've worked really hard today. Well done!

13 The Cross Possum

The TH word family

You will need   T and H alphabet necklaces.

I mouth organ or whistle or similar.

Stories

Possum Magic by Mem Fox. Adelaide (Australia): Omnibus Books, 1983.

See also the Frances series by Russell Hoban, published by Harper & Row (New York): *Bedtime for Frances* (1960), *A Baby Sister for Frances* (1964), *A Birthday for Frances* (1968), *Best Friends for Frances* (1969), *A Bargain for Frances* (1970), etc. Though Frances is a badger and not a possum, the series is charming and worth considering for this lesson.

Today we're going to take a walk in the woods and we'll have a picnic lunch. All pretending of course! But I must warn you that there's a very cross possum where we're going and he'll scratch us if we wake him up. He sleeps all day unless he hears a word with a TH in it.

Hold up two letters on cards left over from the AR lesson.

If we do make a slip and say a word with TH in it, we have to stand very still like tall, tall trees, pretending that we're not there at all.
Can anyone think of a word that begins with TH? Think, thank, the, there, this, that, thought, throne. *Super! What about words with TH in the middle? I know one! Mother! Any others?* Father, brother, bother. *Now how about words ending in TH?* With, bath, moth.

Give a whistle, or a party blower, or a harmonica, or anything that makes a loud noise to one child.

Right, when we all set off I'll do the talking and I'll try to be careful not to say a TH word. But if I do, whoever has the whistle blows once to frighten the cross possum away while we all stand like trees. Let's practice. You blow and we'll all pretend to be trees.

Younger

47

Right, we've got that organized. But what are we going to take on our picnic? You tell me what you'd like to take and why you want to take it.

If the children suggest only food and drinks, you might ask, "What will you sit on? What will you play with? How will you carry it all?" Allow at least five minutes for this information.

Right! We know what we want to take so we'd better get it organized. Remember all the things we'll need? Get them ready and pack them up.

You mime it, too, so that the children know what's expected.

Terrific. I think we can start walking. Remember, if you hear me say a TH word make sure you blow the whistle! Away we go! Walk quietly. Isn't it lovely here today? I can hear birds— can you? And I love the blue sky! The! I said the—oh, I am sorry! Quick, blow! Good—we can go on. I love picnics. So does my sister. Actually, my whole family likes going on picnics—my father, my mother, my grandmother . . .

It's to be hoped that whoever has the whistle blows it without needing a prompt.

Oh look! Millions of ants crawling over a dead snake! Yuk! I guess it isn't really millions, but I bet it's thousands and thousands, don't you? Here's a very tall tree. I'm sure I won't even

be able to put my arms around it. No I can't! Can you? Have a try, some of you. Isn't it huge? It must have a very thick trunk.

(Whisper to the children:)

You're terrific at hearing TH words. I'm scared of Mister Cross Possum so thank you for not waking him up!

We're almost at our picnic spot. It's a beautiful place with rocks and trees near a river. Here we are! Oh, take a look! What a beautiful rock! It looks just like a throne. Oh, I am sorry! I'm so careless. Anyway, we can have our picnic now and I'm pleased! I'm so thirsty, aren't you? I promise I won't talk while we eat and drink.

Mime eating and drinking so that the children know what's expected.

Okay, let's play our games. You could play hopscotch, or ball, or hide-and-seek, or anything else. Find a friend and let me see what games you like playing.

Leave some time for this. If a child is left out, play ball with him or her, in mime of course!

Aaah, what a great day! Look, I'm really scared of possums who get cross, so let's not go home slowly. We'll run back, okay? Pack up your things first. Are you ready? Run!

Whew! We made it. Hey! Do you know why the possum gets cross when he hears TH words? It's because he used to say "pothum" when he was little. He couldn't say "S" and he thought he had a TH in his name. When he found out that he was a possum, and not a pothum, he got really mad. And now he just hates any words with TH in them. Poor old possum! Let's hear a story about a possum.

14 The Thareeck

Review

You will need   A puppet with a badge or a label saying: I AM A THAREECK.

A box containing the following questions on cards:

- Do you live far away?
- Do you have lightning and thunder where you live?
- Do you know what a farm is?
- Do you have a king or a queen in your country?
- Do you know what shoes and socks are?
- Tell us about your father and mother.
- Do you wash yourself in a bath or a shower?
- Do you know how to play hide and seek?
- Do you ever get sick?

2 extra cards with questions:

- Do you like cheese?
- Do you drive a car?

Come and sit by me. We have a visitor today. What is he, I wonder? Who'd like to read his badge? TH-AR-EE-CK. Mr. Thareeck. Now I've met Mr. Thareeck before and I know that he'd love to answer any questions you have. The only problem is that he can only understand a question if there's a TH word, an AR word, a double EE word, or a CK word in it. I've written out a few questions for you to try. When you read out the questions, say the special words very loudly. Like this.

Hold up a card and read it to the class.

Do you like cheese, Mr. Thareeck?

Puppet jerks awake.
(Puppet:)

Yes I do! Hello, hello children! I'm so pleased to mEEt you. Right! Let's try another question.

Hold up "Do you drive a *car*?" Choose a child to ask this question in a loud, clear voice.
(Child:) "Do you drive a *car*?"
(Puppet:)

Older

50

A car? Certainly not! Silly old-fashioned things. No! I fly a deek.

In the following conversation, you and the children try to find out what a deek is. It is anything you can imagine!

Let's have another question.

The pattern for the rest of the lesson is as follows:
A child chooses a question and reads it out.
Mr. Thareeck either explains or asks for clarification.
If clarification is required, the children have to act out or mime whatever it is Mr. Thareeck doesn't understand. For example, if he doesn't know what thunder and lightning are, he can say so. The children will probably say that thunder is noisy. Mr. Thareeck can ask them to make a thunderous noise so that he knows how loud it is. Or, if he doesn't know how to play hide-and-seek, the children can play it to explain it to him.
Play it by ear. The aim of this lesson is to get the children talking to the puppet and then acting out the things he doesn't understand.
(Puppet:)

I must go away now, in my deek. Thank you for giving me such a good time! See you later!

Take puppet off.

What a crazy person! Let's send him a thank-you letter for coming to visit our class today.

15 Rum Dum Dar

Rhyming words

You will need   Blackboard and chalk.

Rum, dum dar, We're rid - ing in a car. We're

rid - ing in a lit - tle car, Rum, dum dar!

Come and sit beside me. What's this place we're in? A room.
Rooms have walls. What rhymes with wall? Tall, small, all,
ball. Yes! I'd like all of you, even the tall ones and the small
ones, to bounce a ball off the wall.

Mime this to show what you mean so that the children don't
think that they should, in fact, have a ball.

While you play I'll sing.

> *Rum dum dall,*
> *I'm playing with my ball.*
> *I'm playing with my super ball,*
> *Rum dum dall.*

I'm wearing a skirt today.

If you're not wearing a skirt (which is likely if you are a male
teacher), a girl in the class is bound to have one on.

What rhymes with skirt? Shirt! Put on a shirt while I sing:

> *Rum dum dirt,*
> *I'm putting on my shirt.*
> *I'm putting on my cotton shirt,*
> *Rum dum dirt.*

All

What color is your shirt?

Ask a few children.

How many buttons are there on your shirt?
Who can tell me two words that rhyme? Bed, Fred. Wonder-ful! Look at this song—it's the one I've been singing, but it's got some words left out. If we were singing about "bed," what might we write into the blank spaces?

This is written on the blackboard.

Rum dum d____
I'm ____ ____ ____ ____
I'm ____ ____ ____ ____ ____
Rum dum ____

The third line is the tricky one, isn't it?

You will end up with something like this:

Rum dum ded,
I'm snuggled in my bed.
I'm snuggled in my lovely bed,
Rum dum ded.

All lie down and snuggle into bed.

Mime this to demonstrate for the children.

We'll all sing our bed song together. "Rum dum ded . . ."
Come and sit by me. What's another rhyme?

You have to be really alert from here on! Whatever words come up, you have to make a song about them, with the children's help, of course. And then you have to mime the activity, so keep the whole thing really simple!

You're great at rhymes! See if you can clap to this rhyme. It's an old playground clapping game.

The children clap their hands together while you speak the rhyme.

My mother said
That I never should
Play with the gypsies
In the wood.
If I did,
She would say,
"Naughty girl to disobey!"

This time, you say it with me. Great! Find a partner. Now we're going to clap on our knees, our chests, and then our partner's palms as the rhyme is said. Slowly now! "My mother said / That I never should . . ."
Super! Sit by me. What rhymes with sun? Fun? Yes! Haven't we had fun today!

16 The Little OR

The OR word family

You will need 2 alphabet necklaces with the letters O and R.

4 cards with an OR word on each:
LORD, LORNA, BORN, and ADORED

15 green water-lily-leaf–shaped cards. On 10 of these cards write an OR word:
BORN, TORN, MORNING, WORN, HORN, CORNER, CORDUROY, STORE, STORM, LORD
Leave 5 waterlily leaf cards blank.

A black felt pen.

Stories

Corduroy by Don Freeman. New York: Penguin/Puffin Books, 1976.

A Pocket for Corduroy by Don Freeman. New York: Penguin/ Puffin Books, 1980.

Sit by me.
  Once upon a time there was a little OR.

  As you tell the story, hold up the O and R and then the words.

  Her father was a rich lord *and her mother was a lady called* Lorna. *From the moment she was* born, *her mother and father* adored *her.*
  One day, when she was six years old, the little OR went for a stroll in the park with her mother and father. She played on the swings and climbed the trees and fed the ducks. She loved the ducks and stayed with them for a long time. When she looked for her parents, she saw them far away on the other side of the duck pond.
  "Oh dear," said the little OR. "How can I get to my mother and father quickly?"
  There was a bridge, of course, but the little OR's eyes were so

All

filled with tears that she didn't see it. Then she heard a whisper. It was the water lilies speaking.

"Step on us! Step on us! We'll help you across, little OR, because we love you."

So the little OR stepped gently on each leaf and, as she did so, she saw that each leaf had her name on it somewhere.

Hold up the leaves one by one.

There was born and torn and worn and horn; morning and corner and corduroy; and storm, store, and lord.

When she reached her parents she told them what she had seen. "They are magic lilies," said her mother. "They have always loved you because you are a little OR and each of them has OR in its name." On the way home the little OR whispered, "Thank you," to each leaf and they smiled and smiled. "We'll never forget you, little OR. We'll never forget you ever."

Let's put the water lilies across this pond. Really gently now, let's step on each one and, as we do so, we'll say the word that's written on it. Make a line and follow me.

As you step on each word, say it. The children follow you one by one, saying the word as they step on it. You all step across one by one. Because you go first, it shouldn't be difficult for the children to say the words after you.

It would be easier if we had more leaves, wouldn't it? I have some here but they haven't got OR words on them. Who can think of a word with OR in it that makes the sound "or"?

Some suggestions: port, shore, sore, boring, for, forget, more.

Would you like to write it on the leaf for us?

Some children may need help here.

We should be able to get back much faster now. Who'd like to go first? I'll go last. Off you go!
Can anyone find me the "corduroy" leaf? And the "corner" one? And "morning"? and "torn"?

Children give you those leaves. As you say the next sentence, hold up the words.

I'm standing in a corner in the morning putting on my torn corduroy jeans.
Let's all say that and do the actions: "I'm standing in a corner in the morning putting on my torn corduroy jeans." Great! Now let's whisper this sentence, except for the OR words. We'll shout those words out loudly. "I'm standing in a CORNER in the MORNING putting on my TORN CORDUROY jeans!"
Great! In class I'll read you another story. This one's about a bear called Corduroy.

Perhaps you could, with the children, write a story about Nora and Norman, the orphans.

Section The World Around Us

The lessons in this section are elementary explorations into science. Piaget claims that children only learn what they themselves create, which is why we have tried in these lessons to involve children on a creative level instead of merely cognitively. Some of the links to science are tenuous but, as a whole, the section opens children's eyes to the world around them.

17 Caterpillars and Butterflies

You will need   A *live* caterpillar in a box with leaves.

A piece of fruit that looks like a caterpillar has been there first.

A butterfly mounted on a piece of board, if possible.

Paper, paint, and scissors for making wings.

Stories

The Very Hungry Caterpillar by Eric Carle. New York: Putnam Publishing/Philomel Books, 1981.

Where Does the Butterfly Go When It Rains? by May Garelick. New York: Young Scott, 1961.

Terry and the Caterpillars by Millicent E. Selsam. New York: Harper & Row, 1962. A Science I Can Read Book.

Music

Light, fluttery music such as "Spring" from *The Four Seasons* by Vivaldi.

There are certain times in the year when caterpillars are easy to find. This lesson is meant for that time of the year!

How do caterpillars move? Let's watch one. I have leaves and a caterpillar here. We'll take the caterpillar out, put it on the leaves, and study the way it moves. Look, one part goes up and then, when that goes down, this part goes up. It's crawling. That looks terribly difficult. Could you put the caterpillar back, please? Thanks. I bet I couldn't move like that. Could you? Let's have a try.
Crawl around like caterpillars.

It's to be hoped you're correctly dressed for this occasion!

You look terrific. Crawl to the end of your leaf and then crawl back to me.

Read *The Very Hungry Caterpillar* to the children. If you read another caterpillar story, tell the children about the very hungry caterpillar who ate through five oranges.

Younger

The very hungry caterpillar eats through five oranges. Honestly! Let's all stand in the middle of the room close together, with our arms around each other. We are all one big orange. Who'd like to be a caterpillar? You'll have to crawl through our legs from one side to the other.

Allow two children at one time to crawl in between the legs. It's fairly chaotic and giggly, but not uncontrollable. Let as many children as possible be caterpillars.

Ugh! I've got holes all through me, just like this rotten fruit here.

Show your fruit.

What happens to the very hungry caterpillar when he's eaten all that food? That's right! He weaves himself into a cocoon.

Show the picture of the cocoon in the book.

Find your space and curl up into a cocoon shape. What's it like in there? It's warm, I bet. Is it noisy? Dead quiet? Can you see anything? Why not? Does it feel really nice? In a minute, when the music starts, you can nibble your way out of that warm cocoon and very gradually unfold your beautiful wings. You'll be a butterfly, as light as a breeze, fluttering from leaf to leaf. Are you ready?

Play the fluttery music.

Beautiful butterflies! Flutter over here. Next time you see a butterfly you'll know that once upon a time it was only a caterpillar just like this one. Let's cut out two butterfly wings and then paint them in class. The colors are fantastic!

It would be marvelous to have a mounted butterfly, if possible, or good, colored pictures to study the wings.

18 Floating and Sinking

You will need   A bowl of water.

A nail.

A cork.

Stories

Who Sank the Boat? by Pamela Allen. New York: Putnam Publishing/Coward-McCann, 1985.

Mr. Gumpy's Outing by John Burningham. New York: Penguin/Puffin Books, 1984.

Mr. Gumpy's Motor Car by John Burningham. New York: Penguin/Puffin Books, 1983.

Music

Light fluttery music such as "Spring" from *The Four Seasons* by Vivaldi.

Heavy elephant music such as "Summer" from *The Four Seasons* by Vivaldi.

Younger

Remember the butterfly lesson? You were terrific. Let's do it again when the music starts. Off you go!

Stop the music.

Can you imagine an elephant trying to fly? Why can't elephants fly? They haven't got wings! Of course. I think it would be really funny to be an elephant trying to fly—would you like to do that? Wait till I find the right music.

Stick to *The Four Seasons.* All you need to do is to change tracks from "Spring" (allegro) to "Summer" (presto). The music for the elephants is really exciting, so let the kids go crazy!

Off you go! Wasn't that fun! I loved being an elephant trying to fly! Let's lie down for a bit of a rest. Find your space and lie on your back. You're floating in a lovely warm sea. The sun's on your face, the water's lapping gently, and your hair is floating. You feel terrific—really warm and calm and restful. All right! Get out of the water and dry yourselves on your big beach towel and come and sit by me.

I have a bowl of water here. If we had a huge, huge bowl of water and we put a big rock in it, what would happen? Why do rocks sink? Because they're heavy. Would a butterfly sink? Why not? OK! I have a nail here. What do you think will happen when it gets put into the water? Who'd like to do it for us? It sank! You were right! Why did it sink? Now here's a cork. Pass it around so that you can all feel it. Will the cork sink? Why not? Let's see you put it in the water.

Pick a child to put the cork in the water.

It's floating! Now I'm going to call out a list of things. If you think they'll float, stand up with your arms out and say, "Aaah!" If you think they'll sink, make yourself into a small ball on the floor and say, "Bong!" Find your space. Are you ready?

Go through the list quickly so that the children are up and down all the time.

- A little fairy ("Aaah")
- A rock ("Bong")
- A water-lily leaf ("Aaah")
- A Popsicle stick ("Aaah")
- A crown with jewels ("Bong")
- A bag of gold ("Bong")
- A feather ("Aaah")
- A letter from Wilma ("Aaah")
- Yourself ("Aaah"—we hope)

Add your own ideas to this list.

I have a lovely story here to finish our lesson today.

19 Sun and Shadow

You will need

A sunny day.

A box with a lid.

2 chairs.

1 table.

Poem

"My Shadow." From *A Child's Garden of Verses* by Robert Louis Stevenson. Illustrated by Michael Foreman. New York: Delacorte Press, 1985.

Save this lesson for a sunny day.

Sit close to me.

(Whisper:)

There's something in this box, but it's too shy to come out. It's a shadow. It said that it might come out at the end of the lesson after it's got used to us. So we'll put it here for safe-keeping.
What is a shadow?

You'll get all sorts of answers.

It's what happens when you or I block the rays of the sun. Trees have shadows. In fact, everything makes shadows. Can you imagine a shadow eating? How would a shadow feel if you jumped on it, or poured cold water on it? It wouldn't feel anything at all, because shadows can't feel. Can we feel shadows? Come outside and find out. Make a shadow and then try to feel it. Can you feel it? No. Can you taste it? I dare you to try—ugh! No. You can only see it. Watch my shadow following me. Look at it! Scaredy-cat! It won't leave me alone. Try to shake off your shadow.
Let's go back inside and I'll read a poem about a really friendly little shadow.

Read "My Shadow" by Robert Louis Stevenson.

Shadows are like the people (or things) that make them. Find a partner. One of you is the person and the other is the

Younger

63

shadow. Whatever the person does, the shadow must copy. You can skip, or play ball, or hang out washing, or have a picnic, or anything—but that shadow has to do it, too! Off you go! Terrific. Now change over to give the other person a turn at being the shadow. Off you go. I'll be the sun shining brightly! Super! Come and sit by me.

Do you know that sometimes shadows are long and other times they're little? It all depends on the time of day. At lunchtime the sun is high in the sky and the shadows are little. In the evening and early in the morning the shadows are long. Where does the sun rise, do you know? In the east! You brilliant child! Of course. And it sets in the . . . ? West!

All find your space. This chair is the east, where the sun gets up, and that chair at the other end of the room is the west, where the sun goes to bed. There's a table in the middle and when the sun is high on that, it's lunchtime. You're going to be long shadows in the morning when the sun gets up; little shadows at lunchtime; and long ones again when the sun goes to bed in the west. I'm going to be the sun.

You crouch on the east chair. Start to rise.

Are the shadows tall? Good.

Run to the table and stand on it.

It's really hot because I'm shining high in the sky at lunchtime. Are the shadows little? Good!

Run to the west chair.

Ooh, I'm sleepy. It's time for me to go to bed. Are the shadows tall again? Good! I love being the sun. This time I think I'll be a shadow. Who'll be the sun?

You and the children change shapes as the sun rises and sets.

I can see the sun rising in the east. It's moving now. Gosh, it's hot! And I'm so small. And now that sleepy old sun is going to sleep in the west and I'm really tall.

Let two more children be the sun.

Excellent! Let's pretend we're at the beach at lunchtime. It's hot! The sun is right overhead. Put on some sunburn lotion. Don't lose the top of it in the sand. Put the top on and rub in the lotion. What about some for your nose? Pick up the tube and squeeze out some lotion. Smear it over your nose and under your eyes. Super!

It's too hot for me! We don't want to get burned, so let's put up an umbrella—a striped beach umbrella. Ooh, it's heavy and it's difficult to put up. There! I've done it. Mine is red and orange. What color is yours? And yours? And yours?

Ask some of the children to tell you the colors of their umbrellas.

Look at the shadow that the umbrella's made. Let's all lie down in it. Aah, that's better.
Come and sit by me. Wasn't it great at the beach?

(Whisper:)

I think our shadow might be brave enough to come out now, don't you? Let's go out into the sun.
Who'll open the box? Very slowly. Thanks. Sssh.

Go outside again to see the shadow the box makes.

Here she comes. Hello, shadow! Thank you for coming out. You must come again. We like you. Let's leave her there till it's time to go home and see what happens. I bet she'll be longer, don't you? See you later, shadow. Bye!

20 Icarus

You will need A candle and some matches.

A model (or toy) airplane.

Blackboard and chalk to show Daedalus' plans as follows:

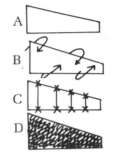

A For one wing, nail four planks together.

B With string, fix willow branches into position.

C Cover with piece of silk. Sew it on.

D Pour hot wax over it all, place feathers on top quickly.

Stories

The story of Daedalus and Icarus. This is a popular legend and can be found in many collections of Greek myths and legends.

Sunflight by Gerald McDermott. New York: Four Winds Press, 1980.

Music

"Hall of the Mountain King" from the *Peer Gynt Suite* by Grieg.

The Sorcerer's Apprentice by Dukas.

Darken the room by pulling curtains if you can. If you can't, the children will suspend disbelief for you.

Sit by me while I light my candle—it's so dark in here.

(Light the candle.)

Each of you has a candle too. Let me see you holding it.

Children mime this.

Older

Make the wick stand up well out of the wax. Splendid! I'd like you to light your candle from mine.

Children mime this.

Hold your candle straight so that the hot wax doesn't drip on your hand. Fantastic!

Now take your candle very carefully, without letting it blow out, to the edge of the room. Blow it out. Take off your shoes and socks and put your candle between your shoes so that you can remember where it is.

Great! Come and sit close to me. What can you tell me about candles?

Talk about candles—what they're for, what kinds there are, etc.

What else gives us light? Electric lights? Yes. Fire? Yes. Remember last week's lesson? The sun! Of course!

Stand up and show me what would happen if you left a candle burning too long. Magnificent! What sad little blobs of wax you are!

Do you remember being an elephant trying to fly? And you couldn't, could you! Well, we can't fly either unless we're in a plane. But once upon a time there was a young man called Icarus who wanted to fly.

Tell or read the story of Daedalus and Icarus. It's a marvelous Greek legend. Here is a summary.

Daedalus was an inventor of great skill who worked for King Minos on the island of Crete. Daedalus had a son called Icarus. Daedalus displeased King Minos. He and Icarus were in danger of losing their lives. They had to escape, but how? They would be caught if they attempted to go by sea. Daedalus invented wings so that they could fly to freedom on another island. They made wings from wood, string, feathers, and wax. Daedalus and Icarus fitted the wings on each other. Daedalus warned Icarus not to fly too close to the sun. Daedalus flew to freedom. Icarus loved flying. He thought he was really great, really clever. He began to show off, to have a good time. He flew higher and higher towards the sun. The wax melted. The wings fell off. Icarus crashed into the sea and drowned.

Reveal Daedalus' plans sketched out on the blackboard.

Daedalus would have drawn his plans with a quill. A quill is a feather that's been sharpened into a pen. He would have had a jar of ink and some thick paper called papyrus, made by flattening the reeds from the river's edge. You are Daedalus. You have your quill, your ink, and your papyrus.

With extreme care, draw your own plans. Don't spill the ink. Measure everything carefully. Blow it dry. Show it to me. Now you can make the wings.

Hold up your wooden hammer. And the box of nails. Nail your four planks together.

Point to your string. Touch your pile of willow branches. Tie the willow to the frame.

Sew on the large piece of silk. As you sew, your thread gets shorter and shorter.

Pour on the hot beeswax and quickly put the feathers in place.

Help each other strap the wings on.

Explain the music: the first part is for flying, the second part for drowning. The children, like Icarus, fly too close to the sun, then fall into the sea. If the children are enjoying this, repeat it. It usually is enjoyed! Let the children go crazy.

Ssshh. Ooh! Guess what?? The room has turned into a damp, dark, dark, cold cave. We are trapped! Like Icarus, we have to escape. There must be a secret door somewhere. Tap the walls. Have you found it? Oh, good! I see a tunnel that we're going to have to go through. Ugh! It's wet. Put your shoes and socks on. Bring your candle to me and light it

(mimed)

from mine

(real)

before you go. I'll see you outside.

The children follow you outside.

Whew! Thank heavens we're out of that! Put your candles in any shadow that you can find.

21 Planet Earth

You will need Tape recorder set up ready to record.

Letter to Space Creatures as follows:

DEAR SPACE CREATURES

WELCOME TO PLANET EARTH. WE ARE HAPPY TO
HAVE YOU HERE. WE WANT TO KNOW ALL ABOUT YOU.
WOULD YOU PLEASE ANSWER OUR QUESTIONS BY
SPEAKING INTO THE MICROPHONE? IF YOU WANT TO
ASK US ANYTHING, YOU CAN. WE WILL ANSWER
YOUR QUESTIONS BY LETTER. WE ARE AFRAID
OF YOU EVEN THOUGH WE BELIEVE THAT YOU ARE
FRIENDLY. THAT'S WHY WE WANT YOU TO
SPEAK INTO THE TAPE RECORDER AND NOT TO
US. HERE ARE OUR QUESTIONS:

1. WHAT KIND OF HOUSES DO YOU LIVE IN ?

2. WHAT DO YOU EAT ?

3. DO YOU HAVE SCHOOLS ? WHAT ARE
   THEY LIKE ?

4. TELL US ABOUT THE PLANTS AND ANIMALS
   ON YOUR PLANET.

5. DO YOU HAVE DIFFERENT SEASONS ? WE
   HAVE SUMMER, AUTUMN, WINTER, AND
   SPRING.

THANK YOU.
   YOURS SINCERELY
THE EARTH PEOPLE

Older

69

Come and sit by me. We are all creatures from another planet. In a minute we're going to get into a spaceship and visit Planet Earth. What do you think we look like? I think we've all got blue noses for a start! What else?

Elicit descriptions from the children, as well as the name of the planet and their own names. Tell them your name.

My name is Helloff—what's yours?

Find your own space. Put on your space suits. Put on your helmets. Move over here and climb into the spaceship.

You lead the way.

Sit down and fasten your safety belts. We all have controls in front of us. Check that all the switches are in the right positions. Check the time on your watch. Start the engine. 10 . . . 9 . . . 8 . . . 7 . . . 6 . . . 5 . . . 4 . . . 3 . . . 2 . . . 1 . . . Blast off!

Oh, this is fantastic! Look how close we are to the moon! Isn't it bright? What else can you see?

Sun? Stars? Meteorites? Flying saucers? Satellites? etc.

We'll soon be landing on Earth. Be careful! The people may not be friendly and things may be different. They probably don't eat trees and they probably don't drink bathwater—still, we'll just have to get used to it, won't we?

Get ready for landing. Check controls. We've arrived! In a minute we're going to explore on our own. Then we'll meet again to tell each other about all the things we've discovered. You may find it difficult to walk. That's because your shoes are really too heavy for Earth's gravity. Are you ready? Let's get out.

As the children explore, you move around saying obvious things like: "The people here are all different colors!" "They've got two legs!" Give them plenty of time to wander with just a little prompting from you to help their observations, if necessary.

Okay! Come over here and let's tell each other what we have discovered. Do you know that their flowers grow up out of the ground instead of down into the ground? Isn't that incredible? What did you notice?

Leave plenty of time for the children to talk. They pick up ideas of what to say from each other.

While I was wandering I found a letter next to this machine. I think they call it a tape recorder, but it looks very old-fashioned to me. Who'd like to open the letter? It says "To the Space Creatures," so I suppose it's for us.

Give the letter to a good reader to open and read. While he or she is reading, make sure the tape recorder is ready to go. Ask children, preferably volunteers, to answer the questions. More than one child can answer each question if you have time.

Now what questions can we ask them? Can you think of anything?

Elicit the questions before you record them.

Good. We'll leave that here because we've got to go home again. I hope we'll get a letter from them soon.

A letter arrives—written by you—a week later. (Don't forget!)

Into the spaceship. Fasten safety belts. Check controls. 10 . . . 9 . . . 8 . . . 7 . . . 6 . . . 5 . . . 4 . . . 3 . . . 2 . . . 1 . . . Blast off!

Home again! It must be time for something to eat. Let's check with the clock. It is! Great. Back to class with me, you crazy blue-nosed Space Creatures!

22 Seeds and Fruit

You will need   1 unpeeled orange—not a navel.

Orange juice and plastic cups (enough for the whole class to have a drink).

Sit by me. You all know what this is—an orange, of course! But do you know what color it was before it ripened? Green! That's right! What was the green orange before it was an orange? A bud! Yes. And before it was a bud? A flower. And the flower grew on the branch of a tree, and before the tree became a tree, it was . . .? A seed! Look at how small a seed is.

Peel the orange and pick out some seeds for the children to look at.

Everyone hold a seed between your fingers.

Mime this. Make sure that the children have a tiny space between their fingers and thumbs, where the seed should be.

Find your space and put your seed down very carefully.
Right! You have a garden in front of you, and a spade, and a hose attached to a tap. Plant your seed very carefully and then water it gently. Off you go. Dig a hole. Put the seed in, with a little water . . . put the soil back . . . and water it again.
Now sit by me. While we wait for our orange tree to grow, let's play "Oranges and Lemons."

> *"Oranges and lemons,"*
> *Say the bells of St Clement's.*
> *"You owe me five farthings,"*
> *Say the bells of St Martin's.*
> *"When will you pay me?"*
> *Say the bells at Old Bailey.*
> *"When I grow rich,"*
> *Say the bells at Shoreditch.*
> *"And when will that be?"*
> *Say the bells at Stepney.*
> *"I'm sure I do not know,"*
> *Says the great bell at Bow.*
> *Here comes a candle*
> *To light you to bed,*
> *Here comes a chopper*
> *To chop off your—head!*

All

72

An arch is formed by two children who agree secretly which will be an orange and which a lemon. All the other children file under the arch. On "Here comes a candle," the children forming the arch bring their arms down on each child filing through —and release him or her except for the one caught on "head." This child has to choose (in a whisper) whether he or she wants to be an orange or a lemon, and then goes behind the appropriate side of the arch. When all the children are on one side or the other, there is a tug of war.

Mime the following as you give the instructions.

Look at our orange trees! They're covered in oranges! Orange trees can be spikey, so take care. Come and get a basket from me and then pick your oranges until your basket is heavy. Ready? Here's your basket. And yours.

Super! This many oranges would squeeze into a great orange juice drink for us all, wouldn't it?

Begin to pour your jug of real orange juice into the plastic cups.

Isn't it absolutely amazing that this tiny seed can grow and grow and end up being orange juice like this, which we can all gulp down? Cheers!

Wasn't that great? Throw the cups into the bin—it's time for class.

23 Seeds and Vegetables

You will need An attractive jar full of chick-peas.

A turnip.

Stories

The Enormous Turnip. Illustrated by Kathy Parkinson. Niles, IL: Albert Whitman, 1985.

"The Turnip" by Aleksei Tolstoy. From *The Fairy Tale Treasury*, edited by Virginia Haviland, illustrated by Raymond Briggs. New York: Dell, 1980.

Sit in a circle and I'll give you each a magic seed.

Give each child a chick-pea.

Hold it in your hand until it warms up. As it gets warm, it will make you grow and grow and grow.

You "grow" to show the children what's expected.

Wonderful. You all look like tall tomato plants. But that's not what we're going to talk about today.

Put your seeds in the jar, one by one. Pass the jar around. We must hear each seed drop or else it will lose its magic. Now lie down on the floor close to the jar, which is in the middle of our circle. When I say, "Go," we're going to blow three times on the jar to make the seeds keep their magic powers. Are you ready? Go!

Blow, blow, blow.

Thanks! Now they're safe.
What's this?

Hold up the turnip.

Can you tell me anything about it? Does it grow on a tree like an orange? What else grows under the ground? Carrots? Yes! Peas? No! Potatoes? Yes! Onions? Yes! Good. What vegetables grow above the ground? Beans, peas, broccoli, lettuce, tomatoes, peppers, cabbage. Fantastic.

Here's a story about the biggest turnip ever. It was about fifty times bigger than this one.

All

74

Show the turnip to the children.

Tell the story and, as you do, choose a child to be the farmer at the point when he pulls and pulls and pulls. Then choose other children at the appropriate times to be the farmer's wife, the little girl, the dog, the cat, and the mouse. Add ants to the mouse so that the rest of the class can be in on the final pull.

Over we go! Let's have a look at the turnip. Isn't it big? It's all covered in dirt—you can hardly see that it's purple and white. It's going to feed a lot of people, that turnip.

Right! Sit down in a group with two or three other people. Remember that potatoes also grow underground? It's nearly time to go. But you can only go when you're "out" in this next game. One person in each group put up a hand. You have to touch the other children's fists with yours as we sing the rhyme. Everyone put your fists in front of you. I'm sure you all know this.

> One potato, two potato,
> Three potato, four.
> Five potato, six potato,
> Seven potato, more.
> O-U-T spells OUT!

Out you go. You can sit on the floor over there.

Keep saying the rhyme until all the children are out except the leaders. Then you do it to them, all saying the rhyme together until the bitter end and everyone is out.

24 The Five Senses

You will need 6 chairs (if you work in a small room).

12 chairs (if you work in a large room).

Stories

Helen Keller: Toward the Light by Stewart and Polly Anne Graff. New York: Dell, 1965; reprinted 1983.

Helen Keller by Margaret Davidson. New York: Scholastic, 1973.

Sit by me and tell me what ears are for. Would it matter if we didn't have ears? If you couldn't hear, what difference would that make to you?

Have a long discussion.

Today we're going to explore the five senses. Hearing is one of them. Does anybody know any others? What about the sense that we use our eyes for? Seeing! Of course. Our tongue? Tasting, right! Our fingers? Touching. And who can guess the last one? Smelling! Right. Let's go through them again. You show me the ears when I say "Hearing," and so on. Touching. Tasting. Smelling. Seeing. Hearing. Great!

See if you can guess what I'm saying—you'll have to watch carefully.

Mime holding a glass and drinking. Then mouth the words "This is a drink," and point to the glass.

What did I say? It's difficult, isn't it, when you can't hear. Who else would like to mime something and then mouth a few words about it?

Watch one or two.

Find a partner, but don't move yet. One of you is going to be deaf and the other one is going to ask something or tell something without speaking aloud. See if you can understand each other. Find a space.

You go around and do some wild guessing too. Leave the children enough time to warm up in their roles.

All

Magnificent. Let's see a few.

Some children demonstrate in front of the class.

It must be awful to be deaf. Not hearing songs, or stories, or TV, or even what your friends say.

In front of you is a surprise drink. We're going to use our sense of taste this time. I have a drink too. Will it taste nice or nasty? Will I know what it is or not? Tell me what's in your glass. Drink up.

Mime this to show the children what you want them to do.

I can tell by some faces that it tasted good! What was your drink? And yours? Are you sure? Give me a taste, then. You're right! Yummy. You made a face when you swallowed yours. What was it? And yours? Mine was medicine—a terrible cough medicine for wheezy chests. Revolting!

Okay. Now let's think about our sense of touch. I'd like you to touch the floor and another five very different things in this room. Remember what they are. Do it before I count to 10! Go! 1 . . . 2 . . . 3 . . . 4 . . . 5 . . . 6 . . . 7 . . . 8 . . . 9 . . . 10! Marvelous. What did you touch? Can we think of any words to describe how the floor felt when you touched it? Splintery? Rough? Hard?

Go through the objects that a few children touched. Try to use the most evocative adjectives that might later appear in their writing.

Now, what do you know about our sense of smell? I like smelling flowers and perfume but I hate the smell of manure. Can you think of a time when it might be dangerous if you didn't have a sense of smell?

Fire, gas, burning rubber in a car, etc.

With a partner, think up a little play to show me how one person uses his or her sense of smell to save someone's life. I'll give you at least five minutes to think up a scene and practice it.

Help those who appear to be floundering.

Great! Come over here and let's see them.

Pick five to watch. Discuss the implications of being able to smell.

We've looked at smell and taste, touch and hearing. What's the last sense? Sight! Right! Let's put a whole lot of chairs in the middle of the room. Find a partner. One of you is a blind old auntie or uncle. The other one is someone who can see. Auntie must close her eyes while the other person very carefully guides her safely through the chairs. The room's in an old, ruined house. Away you go. Be really careful. You like your auntie . . .

Marvelous—you all got through without too much injury. Do you know there was once a little girl who had all her five senses when she was born. She could hear, see, taste, touch, and smell. But when she was two, she was very ill. She lost her sight and became blind. And she lost her sense of hearing and became deaf. Can you imagine that? I'll go on with my story while you squeeze your eyes shut and block your ears.

Don't speak at all.

Open your eyes! Unblock your ears! Wouldn't it be terrible to be deaf and blind at the same time! This girl's name was Helen Keller. In the end she learned to speak through her sense of touch—by feeling the throat muscles of her teacher and trying to copy it. Isn't that wonderful?

25 The Five Senses Adventure

You will need

A room that can be darkened.

A candle and matches.

A flashlight covered with red cellophane.

A water mister (like a plant spray).

A jar (or a small bowl) with a lid, filled with warm water with liniment (Vicks VapoRub or similar) in it.

Air freshener spray.

Tape recorder, set up to play.

Starting pistol.

Crackers or nuts for everyone.

Music

Flute music.

Come and sit close to me.	Speak in hushed tones.
Once upon a time, a long time ago, there lived an old magician deep inside a dark wood. Oh, it was very, very dark. Oh, it was very dark indeed.	Turn off lights. Draw curtains. Then light the candle with a shaking hand.
Sometimes, it is true, there was a red glow from the magician's fire.	Shine the torch.
When it rained, the old man would warm his hands around his magic pot.	Spray the children with water squirter. Pass around jar with warm water inside it. Make sure that lots of children have a turn at warming their hands around the "magic pot."
Sometimes he would open the pot and sniff deeply at the magic potion.	Take off the lid of the jar so that the smell of liniment pervades the air.

All

And then he would say his magic chant, which was always repeated by anyone who happened to hear it—almost as if the mystery of the chant forced people to say it after him.

> Ming ha do doopey day,
> Ming ha do doopey day.
> I'll make a spell today,
> And who knows, who can say,
> What this small spell will do
> For me or even you?
> Ming ha do doopey day,
> Ming ha do doopey day.

And then he would repeat the last two lines, clapping for every word.

One bright morning, when the birds were singing and the flowers were smelling sweetly, the magician felt a creepy feeling in his spine and his hair tingled as if something was about to happen.

Whistle, tweet, or both. Spray the freshener around. Creep your fingers up a few spines near you. Touch hair with creepy fingers.

He listened very carefully. He strained to hear something. What was it? A flute. It must be his great friend, Raphael. He decided to walk to meet him. He wanted to surprise him so he walked very quietly.

Long, long tense pause. Turn on tape faintly.

He crept through the forest without a sound. The flute seemed nearer. The magician was glad he would see his friend soon. What was that?

Get up. Inch forward. Turn up volume.

A gun. It was a trick. It was not his friend. It was not Raphael. It was the bandits—the wicked men who lived in the caves in the hills. In great fear the magician fumbled in his pockets for his magic pills.

Fire the starting pistol. Turn music off.

He put a tablet in his mouth. He ate the tablet at once. That would save him from the bandits—the wicked men from the caves in the hills.

Put a cracker or nut in each child's mouth.

80

Oh, how happy he was! He hugged himself. He hugged everything around him, including the trees and bushes in the forest. As he walked back, he felt that he had to take deep breaths and let them out little by little. It was the old magician's way of laughing.

Do it! Hug the children and encourage them to hug each other.

He took in a deep breath and let it out with three laughs.
He laughed again and again until he was rolling around the floor of his little hut in laughter.

Take a deep breath. Laugh like the magician.

Roll on floor, laughing in this way.

Then he felt tired and everything around him felt tired. Pretty soon the forest and everything in it fell into a long and beautiful sleep.

Lie down. Sleep. Play the tape softly. When it finishes, wake up.

Oh, goodness. I feel as if we've been in another world, don't you? What's all this stuff lying around? We'd better tidy this place up. Can you help me?

81

26 Solids, Liquids, and Gases

You will need 1 orange ice cube tray (empty).

A tambourine.

A triangle.

Music

Music with heavy and light contrasts such as *Piano Concerto in C*, K467 (the *Elvira Madigan* theme) by Mozart, or electronic music.

Come and sit by me.

Show the empty ice cube tray.

Tell me all you can about this. It's plastic. It's orange. It has hollow sections in it for water. It goes into the freezer. The water gets hard and becomes ice. Right. Up and down the length of this room is a big ice cube tray. Let's all sit in our own little section of it. We're water. Someone's putting us all into the freezer. We're getting colder and colder. When I'm freezing I shall be so frozen I won't be able to talk. I'm frozen.

Stand up, as teacher.

Can I see if you're frozen? You should be so stiff that I can't move a finger, or a head, or anything.

Test a few children for "frozen" qualities.

Right. I'm taking you out of the freezer and I'm putting all the ice cubes in a saucepan. I'm lighting the gas underneath and you're going to melt. M-E-L-T.

Water freezes into ice in the freezer and it melts when it is outside the fridge. If we put water on a gas stove and let it boil, what happens? What do you see? What makes a kettle whistle? Steam! What's the difference between ice and steam? If we were all stiff and still when we were ice, could you show me what steam would be like? Off you go!

Play the music.

This time when I bang loudly on my tambourine, you're going to be ice. When I play the triangle, you can be water and

Younger

move in a relaxed way. But when the music comes on, you'll be steam—as light as air, all over the place! Are you ready?

Play the triangle, tambourine, triangle, music, triangle, tambourine.

You look terrific! Come and sit by me. We have some useful words to describe ice, water, and steam. Ice is a solid. Solids keep their shape. But when you melt ice, it will change to water. Water is a liquid. Liquids flow and pour. If you heat the water and let it boil, it will change to steam. Steam is a gas. A gas has no shape at all. Solids, liquids, and gases are three kinds of matter. Anything that has weight and takes up room is matter. Matter is made up of millions of tiny molecules moving about. In ice, these molecules are close together because ice is a solid. In water, these molecules are further apart because water is a runny liquid. In steam, they are far apart from each other because they're a gas floating in the air.

Come and stand in the middle of the room. Let's all be the molecules in ice. Stand as close together as you can. Closer. Closer. Super! Now be really stiff. You're ice! What a beautiful solid you are, you are, what a beautiful solid you are!

Now let's be water. Let's be the molecules in water. They're not too cold and they're not too hot. Stand a bit apart from each other. You're the molecules in water. What a beautiful liquid you are, you are, what a beautiful liquid you are!

Of course, you guessed! Now we're going to be the molecules in steam. Boy! Are you boiling! Get as far away from everyone else as possible. Further. Further. Very good! What a beautiful gas you are, you are, what a beautiful gas you are!

This time when I bang the tambourine you'll all be a solid, packed tightly together in the middle of the room. When I play the triangle you can be liquid. I think you might sway a bit as a molecule in liquid, don't you? And when the music comes on you'll be gas, moving around the room as far from anyone else as possible. Are you ready? Off you go.

Bang the tambourine, play the triangle, play the music, play the triangle, bang the tambourine, play the triangle, etc. Children love it!

Section  Our Community and Where We Live

In these lessons, children learn about
people and places through drama, songs,
actions, and games. It is a fun way to
find out what people in our community
do for us.

27 The Doctor

You will need   A real stethoscope.

A real prescription pad.

Pencils and paper for the whole class.

A medicine glass and medicine spoon.

IMPORTANT: Do *not* tell the class what this lesson is about before you begin.

Today I am going to divide you into two groups. I am going to whisper to Group A and ask them to pretend to be someone you all know. Group B has to try to guess who it is.

Divide the class in half at opposite ends of the room. Whisper to Group A that they are going to pretend to be doctors. Tell them to think up and mime some actions that doctors do. Now, ask them to find a space and wait until you tell them to begin. Tell Group B to sit quietly and watch.

All right. Begin.

Group B will probably guess fairly quickly. If they do, suggest that some of the "doctors" show the class what they were doing. Now ask the class to sit near you. Talk about going to the doctor.

What happens when you go to the doctor? Tell me about her office. What does she wear? Oh! You have a man doctor, do you? What's he like? What do you have to do to become a doctor?

Usually there are some interesting answers here.

You have to study—that's right. You go to a university for six to eight years. That's as long as you have been alive! At the university you read lots of big, heavy books and you must remember everything in them. And guess what else? You may have to cut up dead bodies to find how our insides work. Yuk!

Now, find your space and pretend that you have a dead body to cut up. Take your scalpel—that is the very sharp knife that doctors use—and cut all the way down the middle. Ooh, there's an awful smell, isn't there? What have you found inside? A heart! Let's see. Clever you! Can everyone else find the heart?

Older

Point to where the heart is.

I can feel something else, lots of things that are hard, not soft. What can they be? Bones, probably. Ribs, I should think.

Point to your ribs.

This is revolting. I can't go on. Leave the dead bodies and wash your hands. There are faucets, soap, and a wash basin close to you.

Mime these actions yourself in front of the children.

Dry your hands and come and sit by me.
What does the doctor wear around her (or his) neck? A steth-oscope. That's a really difficult word to say, isn't it? Steth-o-scope. Listen to this stethoscope song.

Sing the stethoscope song to the tune of "The more we are together."

> *I wish I had a stethoscope,*
> *A stethoscope, a stethoscope,*
> *I wish I had a stethoscope,*
> *To hear your heart beat.*
> *I'd listen and listen,*
> *And listen, and listen,*
> *I wish I had a stethoscope,*
> *To hear your heart beat.*

Let's all sing it together, slowly.

Sing the song together, slowly at first and then faster.

Guess what I have? A real stethoscope. Who'd like to listen?

Let a few of the children listen with the stethoscope. Tell them that since you will have it with you all day the rest can have their turns later.

If you have a really awful cold and cough, and you feel hot and miserable, what does the doctor tell you to do to get better?

Emphasize the point that the doctor gives you a prescription and not the actual medicine. Or that she (or he) might just send you home to bed.

If you need medicine, the doctor will write out a prescription for it. A prescription pad looks like this. The doctor writes down the name of the medicine you need and how often you have to take it. Then what happens? You take your prescription to the druggist, who puts the medicine into a bottle and you pay for it.
Let's all be doctors. Here's a pencil and some paper. We are all going to write out a prescription. Put your name at the top. Write away. Can I have your prescriptions, please?

Gather up the pencils and prescriptions.

On the prescription the doctor writes the name of the medi-cine you need to take to get better. You usually take medicine about four times a day after meals and before going to bed, for about five days. Sometimes you have to have tablets instead. How do you take tablets?

Talk about tablets you chew or those you take with water.

Now I'm going to be the doctor. I'm going to give each of you a prescription. You go to the druggist over there and buy your medicine. When you have paid for it, come back here to me and sit down. Here are your prescriptions.

Hand out the ones that the children wrote and give them time to act out going to the druggist.

Now I suppose some of you have pills and some of you have syrupy medicine. If you have syrup, you need a medicine glass like this, or a special measuring spoon.

Show the medicine glass and spoon.

I want to guess what each of you is taking—tablets or syrupy medicine.

Watch the children individually for a while, then all together, as it can take too long to see every child.

Now you have to guess what I am taking.

Mime having syrup from a medicine glass.

What's this?

Hold up stethoscope.

What's this?

Hold up medicine glass or spoon or bottle.

What's this?

Hold up prescription pad.

You are brilliant! You have learned about three difficult words today. Now listen to this song.

Sing to the tune of "Twinkle, Twinkle, Little Star," with a slight change of beat.

> *Stethoscope, prescription,*
> *And medicine—*
> *These are the words*
> *That we can say.*
> *Stethoscope, prescription,*
> *And medicine—*
> *Those are the words*
> *We learned today.*

Let's sing it all together.
Now it's time for class. Let's pretend that we have a sore foot and the doctor has put a bandage around it. Don't get the bandage dirty!

28 The Mail Carrier

You will need   A post box (a red cardboard box with a slit for letters).

Old envelopes, postcards, window envelopes, magazines, etc.

4 parcels (wrapped packets of crackers).

4 shoe boxes arranged 2 above and 2 below for sorting mail. Write the name of a nearby town on each.

A large piece of paper.

A thick felt-tipped pen.

A large envelope.

A 22-cent stamp.

A pillowcase.

A large box of crackers (or similar).

A list of place names (towns, cities) familiar to the children (one place name per child).

Let's write a letter to someone! Whom shall we write it to? Wilma? Giant John? Your mother?

Choose someone to write a letter to.

I have a big piece of paper here so that you can see the words I write. We'd better put our address in this corner like this:

Write your school's address in the top right-hand corner.

Do you know what the zip code is for our school? It's important to put the zip code because it helps the people in the sorting office to send our letter to the right place. Our zip code is _ _ _ _ _.

Write it.

Underneath our address we put today's date. What's the date today? That's right! We write the day, then the month, and finally the year. Super! Now we can start.

Let the children dictate a short letter about something exciting they've done recently. Allow them all to sign it. Then address an envelope—the biggest one the school can provide—and put a real stamp on it.

Older

Super! Who'd like to mail that letter in our mailbox over there?

"Over there" is a red painted cardboard box, a fairly big one, with a slit in the appropriate place.

Let's think about all the things that are mailed. We've just mailed a letter. What else do people mail?

If the children can't guess, show them a little parcel, a window envelope for bills, a magazine, and an airmail letter. Otherwise, show them examples of the things we mail as you talk about them.

You're going to mail something soon. Will it be a postcard, or an airmail letter in an envelope, or a bill, or a parcel, or an ordinary letter? I'd like to be able to guess. You'd better first think of whom you're going to send it to. Find your own space. Here's my pen and paper.

Mime actions now.

Have you got yours? Start writing.

Wander around and chat to the children about whom they're writing to, whether they've remembered their own address and the date, what they've written so far, what sort of letter they're writing, etc.

Right. Now mail your letters in our mailbox.

The children mime mailing their letters into the red cardboard box.

After the letters have been mailed, they are collected in a bag.

Empty the mailbox yourself. Put all the old envelopes, parcels, etc. into a pillowcase.

They are then taken to the sorting office.
I'm taking the letters to the sorting office in my red post office van.

Zoom around the room.

At the sorting office, the letters are sorted into little boxes like this.

Arrange the four shoe boxes in front of you, two on top and two on the bottom, so that they look like pigeonholes. Give each box the name of a nearby suburb or town. I have used suburbs I know for this example. Just substitute your own.

I'm going to sort the mail. This letter is for Blackwood . . . , Eden Hills, Bedford Park, Bellevue Heights, Bedford Park, Eden Hills, Eden Hills, Blackwood, Eden Hills, etc.

"Sort" all the letters.

Now I need four mail carriers—one for each town.

Give out the appropriate pile of letters to each of the four mail carriers.

Now I need people to live in those places.

Ask the children to sit in lines of approximately six "houses" each.

Okay, mail carriers! This is Blackwood. This is Eden Hills. This is Bellevue Heights, and this is Bedford Park. Deliver your letters by dropping them into pretend mailboxes near each house.

The children deliver the letters. Make sure you have arranged the mail sorting so that at least one parcel goes to each town.

Super! Sit over here and let's see what you received.

Ask the children about the letters and parcels they received.

Who received parcels? Open them! Crackers! Ah, lucky you! You'd better eat them. They are for you, after all. Who didn't get a parcel? You can have some of mine.

Share a box of crackers among those who missed out.

Review the words: address, postcard, date, sorting office, etc., using the examples the children now have.

We're going to play a game called "General Delivery" now. Everyone sit in a circle. You are all places.

Using your list of place names, give each child a place to be around the circle.

Now, who'll be our first mail carrier? Come here and be blindfolded.

Select a child to be the first mail carrier.

When I say, "The mail is going from one place to another," those two people change places. The mail carrier then has to try to catch one of them as they do. The mail carrier then becomes the place name of whomever he or she caught. The person caught then becomes the mail carrier. Okay? Are you ready?

Name places on your list.

Play the game for as long as it is fun. If you have a large group, you may need to go over the place names two or three times.

Great. It's time for class. I'll mail the letter that we all wrote together, and we'll see if we get an answer.

29 The Baker

You will need Fresh yeast.

A pie tin.

Biscuit cutters.

Unleavened bread (like Lebanese bread).

Stories

In the Night Kitchen by Maurice Sendak. New York: Harper & Row, 1970.

The Giant Jam Sandwich by John Vernon Lord and Janet Burroway. Boston: Houghton Mifflin, 1973.

The Gingerbread Man by Fran Hunia. Troy, MI: International Book Center/Ladybird Books, 1977.

"The Gingerbread Boy" by Sara Cone Bryant. From *The Fairy Tale Treasury*, edited by Virginia Haviland, illustrated by Raymond Briggs. New York: Dell, 1980.

Sit by me and we'll say this rhyme together.

> The Queen of Hearts,
> She baked some tarts,
> All on a summer's day.
> The knave of hearts,
> He stole those tarts,
> And took them right away.

And let's all sing this one.

> Sing a song of sixpence
> A pocket full of rye!
> Four and twenty blackbirds
> Baked in a pie.
> When the pie was opened
> The birds began to sing!
> Wasn't that a dainty dish
> To set before the king?

Older

Have you ever thought about who bakes the pies and tarts and bread and rolls for our lunches? What are the people who do the baking called? Bakers! Bakers bake all night so that we can

94

have fresh bread and pies every day. We're going to be bakers in a minute, so we'd better think about what it is that they do.

What do you need to make bread? Measuring cups, flour, yeast, water, salt, a bowl, a wooden spoon, a baking tin, and a hot oven. Right. Have you ever smelled yeast? Have a smell!

Let the children smell the yeast.

It tastes vile. What does yeast do? Well, if you don't know, let me tell you that bread without yeast is flat.

If you live in an area where Lebanese bread is available, show it as an example of unleavened bread.

Find your own space.

Mime making the bread so that the children know what to do and can follow suit.

Get your measuring cups. Measure about 5 cups of flour and put it into your bowl. Crumble the yeast into a cup and pour warm tap water onto it. Stir it till it's all mixed. Add a teaspoon of salt to the flour and stir. Half fill a milk carton with

*warm water. Now pour the yeast into a well in the flour. Stir it
in. Add the rest of the water, little by little, and keep stirring.
Super! Now sprinkle a little flour on the table. Take your dough
and knead it like this. Use the base of the palm of your hand.
Knead it and fold it in half. Knead it again and fold it in half
again. Now we'll put it into a baking tin and cover it with a
clean towel and wait for it to rise. It takes about an hour, which
is too long for us to wait. The yeast makes the bread rise and
rise to the top of the tin. Now we can pop it into our hot oven.
And in about 45 minutes we'll have to take it out because it
will be ready.*

*What other things do we bake? Cakes, biscuits, and pies. Pies
have fruit or custard in them and they are cooked in tins like
this.*

Show a pie tin.

*Biscuits are cut out with cutters like this one and then they
are cooked on flat pans. Cakes have to be frosted. Bakers must
be busy.*

*Choose something that you'd like to bake. If you don't know
the exact recipe, don't worry. Don't burn yourself on your
ovens, that's all I ask. Okay, bakers—find your own space and
bake me something good.*

Allow the children a fair amount of time. Walk around with a
few reminders like: Have you stirred it well? Did you remember
to turn on your oven? Did you forget the salt? Can I help? etc.

*Come and sit down with your goodies. What did you make?
How did you make it? And you . . . And you . . .*

Ask about ingredients and methods.

*Everyone give someone else a bite of what you have made.
Yum! You're really clever, all you bakers. Of course in a big
bakery they have huge bowls and massive ovens and machines
to do the kneading. It must be tiring work. All the bakers in this
town are probably fast asleep at this moment.*

You have a little snooze while I whisper this rhyme:

> *Pat-a-cake, pat-a-cake, baker's man,*
> *Bake me a cake as fast as you can;*
> *Pat it and prick it and mark it with (T)*
> *And put it in the oven for (Tommy) and me!*

Choose the name of a child in the class whose initial rhymes
with "me" (B, C, D, E, G, P, T, V). You may repeat the rhyme,
of course, if you want to!

I have a story to read you in class about baking.

30 The Trash Collector

You will need **Music**

Fast and lively music such as Stephane Grappelli's (the jazz violinist) or Mazurka in B Flat, Op. 7, No. 1 by Chopin, or "I Love Trash" from *Sesame Street*, Volume 1.

Come and sit by me. On your lap you have some hot french fries wrapped up in paper. Hold one up. Ooh, it's hot. Eat it. Yum. You eat yours and I'll eat mine. Don't you just love them? Can I have one of yours? Thanks.

You are a litterbug, you wicked thing. You have left the french-fry wrapping in the street. I'd like you to be that piece of paper. Lie down in your space. When the music starts, the wind is going to blow you all over the street. Are you ready?

Play anything fast and lively. Grappelli, the jazz violinist, has some fantastic records and tapes from which to choose a fast track. For this particular lesson I don't use Grappelli; I use Chopin's *Mazurka in B Flat*, Op. 7, No. 1. But Grappelli may be easier to get ahold of.

Stop the music, or if it's a short piece let it finish. The Mazurka takes less than 2½ minutes.

Right! The wind has gone now. I don't like litter so I'm going to roll you up into a tiny ball. Can you roll yourself up? R-O-L-L. Good. You're small enough to be dropped into the trash can. In you go! What's in the can with you? Take a look.

You can come out of your smelly trash can now. What did you have in there with you?

Talk about what else was in the trash can.

We make trash. What sort of trash do you make in your family?

Ask the children. Elicit the difference between trash that can be burned in an incinerator (e.g., paper, garbage) and nonburnable trash (glass, tins, plastic, etc.).

Show me on your face the smell of your trash. Ugh! Horrible, isn't it? What on earth would you do if we couldn't get rid of our trash? What would happen?

Smell, flies, germs, mess, illness, disease, etc.

All

Flies just love trash, don't they? Find your own space. Some-

97

one's dog has tipped over the trash can, and you're going to be a fly buzzing around it. When I say, "Buzz," you can flit from one thing to another, buzzing busily. Are you ready? Spread your germs. Buzz! Buzz, you horrible fly. Now I'm going to spray you to death.

Make a spray noise.

Ppssshhh! Die, you horrible things!
Now let's be maggots crawling on garbage. Maggots are the babies of flies. They're white fat things, like revolting worms. Crawl away! You're all fat and white and awful, and I wish you weren't in my garbage. I feel sick just looking at you! Crawl away!
Now come and sit by me. Tell me about the people who take our trash and garbage away.

Elicit the speed at which trash collectors work, the clothes they wear, the weights they have to lift, and what we'd do without them. How often do they come? Do they come on the same day every week? Try to instill through conversation a real appreciation of the useful and necessary work these trash collectors do.

Would you like to be a trash collector? Tell me why.
I know someone on TV who adores trash. He even lives in a trash can. Who is he? Oscar the Grouch, on Sesame Street— that's right.

Play the track "I Love Trash," from *Sesame Street*, Volume I. All join in on the chorus.

I feel dirty after that lesson. I bet trash collectors feel dirty, too, after a day's work. Let's all have a shower. Take your clothes off and wash yourselves really well. Even your hair. Rinse it well. Dry yourselves. Get dressed in your best clothes. Super! Now we all look special, all clean and nicely dressed, ready to go visiting.

31 Families

You will need Family photographs showing your relations or the different generations of a family.

Stories

The Story of Ping by Majorie Flack. New York: Penguin/Puffin Books, 1977.

Alex's Bed by Mary Dickinson. North Pomfret, VT: Andre Deutsch, 1980.

Ernest & Celestine by Gabrielle Vincent. New York: Morrow, 1982.

That Is That by Jeanne Whitehouse Peterson. New York: Harper & Row, 1979.

The number of single-parent families can make this lesson fairly difficult to handle. Be aware that in some schools, well over half the children come from homes other than the mom-dad-and-two-kids-living-happily-ever-after type. I have photos of different generations of my family, even of my great-grandfather, which I use. Children are fascinated. Find photos of at least four of your relations, if possible.

Discuss the photographs with the children, talking about parents, grandparents, brothers and sisters, cousins, uncles, and aunts. Try to think up little anecdotes. Look for likenesses, etc.

Tell me about your family. And yours. And yours.

Encourage the children to talk about their own cousins, aunts, uncles, and grandparents; where they live; the number of children in their family; etc.

Did you know that:

All

> *There was an old woman*
> *Who lived in a shoe.*
> *She had so many children,*
> *She didn't know what to do!*
> *She gave them some broth*
> *Without any bread,*
> *Then whipped them all soundly*
> *And sent them to bed!*

Most mothers aren't that mean, are they? Parents can be mean sometimes, though, particularly when they are rushing around in the morning, or when things are carelessly left lying around on the floor.

With three of your friends, act out a scene that shows what happens in your house in the morning.

Allow plenty of time for the scene.

I have a story here about families.

Read the story you have selected.

Have you got uncles and aunts and cousins? Here's a song about Cousin Peter who comes to visit.

Sing the first verse of "Cousin Peter." It's really easy. You could say it, I suppose, if you had to!

Last eve - ning Cous - in Pe - ter came, Last

eve - ning Cous-in Pe - ter came, Last eve-ning Cous-in

Pe - ter came To say that he was here.

Now let's all sing that verse together.

Sing the first verse with the class.

Last evening Cousin Peter came,
Last evening Cousin Peter came,
Last evening Cousin Peter came
To say that he was here.

He hung his hat upon a peg,
He hung his hat upon a peg,
He hung his hat upon a peg
To show that he was here.

While he was here Cousin Peter did all sorts of things.

He wiped his shoes upon the mat, etc.

He kicked his shoes off one by one, etc.

He danced about in his stocking feet, etc.

He played he was a great big bear, etc.

He tossed us up into the air, etc.

He made a bow and said goodbye, etc.

Children can mime the actions suggested by the words.

Who has a girl cousin? What's her name? Let's sing the first verse again with her name.

32 Your Country

You will need A good map of the United States (or Canada), showing the main cities.

A tambourine.

Come sit by me. The world is a big place. Who has been away from home on vacation? Who has ever lived in another country or city?

Encourage the children to talk as much as they want about where they've been and what they've seen. Some will have never left their home town while others may have traveled to other countries.

We're in a room, aren't we? And the room is in a school. The school is in a street. Which street? But what is the street in? A city or town. Terrific. What town do you live in? And you? And you? Can anyone tell me the names of any cities or towns anywhere in the world? What are towns and cities in? Countries. Right. And countries are in the world. And the world is in the universe.
The United States also has states. What are the main cities in each state?

Use local states here. Try for the largest cities in the surrounding area.

Does anyone know the name of the main city, or capital, of the United States? Washington. Where is Washington? Right. It's in the District of Columbia, which isn't a state.

Organize the children into groups representing the states near their home state. Tell each group what state they are representing and the name of its capital city. Each group will stand out front and introduce itself to the others, saying what state or country the group is representing and what the name of the capital city is.

Let's start with (home state).

Each group takes its turn.

Don't forget where you live. Come over here. I want to show you something.

Older

102

Gather round a very clear map of the United States.

Can a person from (state) find (state) for me? And (city)? Super.

Go through the surrounding states so that each group can at least place where it comes from.

Is (city) the capital of (state)? No? Show me the capital of (state). (City), of course! Silly me.

Wouldn't it be lovely to visit the other places? We're going to drive around the United States. When you hear me bang on the tambourine, find another person and say, "Hello, I'm from (state) and my capital is (city). How about you?" And your friend will say where he or she comes from, and what the capital city is. Okay? Off we go.

Bang on the tambourine about six times.

Let's look at this map again. As I point, see if you can name the state and its capital.

Give the children extra practice at finding the city.

Do you remember how we started off? In a room, in a school. What came next? A street in a town or a city. And then? A state in a country, in the world, in the universe. Let's say it all together, starting with a whisper and ending with a shout. Ready?

> *We are*
> *in a room*
> *in a school*
> *in a street*
> *in a city (town)*
> *in a state*
> *in a country*
> *in the world*
> *in the universe!*

(You may have to adapt this to suit your locality if you live in a small town.)

This helps children to realize how small their immediate environments are.

Let's pretend we've been on vacation in another place and we're going to fly back home now.

See lesson 15, page 52 for the tune.

> *Rum dum dane,*
> *We're going home by plane.*
> *We're flying home to (name your town/city),*
> *Rum dum dane.*

Are you ready? Then let's sing our way home. Rum dum dane, etc.

Section V Happenings

Happenings are fantastic. Being more child-oriented than the previous lessons, they are most likely to lead to language development. For language to develop we need to have a purpose: a need to speak, listen, read, or write and a sympathetic audience to interact with. These lessons should provide just that.

It is impossible to give instructions for happenings because the whole idea is that different classes will take off in different directions. Instead, I describe three happenings in which I was involved: "The Angry Gnome," "A Ghost from the Past," and "Queen Meany." Then I suggest some possible starting points for another happening: "The Witch Who Wouldn't Wake Up." A single happening may last as long as an entire term.

Basically the stage for a happening is set by an imaginary character who writes to, telephones, or sends the class a prerecorded tape. What happens next is up to you and the children.

You will need an assistant to play the part. Whom will you be able to persuade to do it? Ah! There's the rub!

33 The Angry Gnome

An ex-student of mine had a very noisy class of five-year-olds in their first year of real school. One morning, the class received a letter under their classroom door. It said something to this effect:

DEAR GRADE ONES IN ROOM SIX

MY NAME IS **KNOBBLY GNOME.** I'M REALLY MEAN AND BAD-TEMPERED. I LIVE IN THE CEILINGS OF YOUR SCHOOL AND I TRY TO SLEEP IN THE DAY TIME. YOU MAKE SO MUCH NOISE, YOU HORRIBLE CHILDREN, THAT I CAN'T SLEEP. SO PLEASE KEEP QUIET, **OR ELSE!**

YOURS SINCERELY

KNOBBLY

The class was amazed, scornful, scared, and excited, all at once. A discussion followed about what they could do. They decided to try to be quieter for a week and then to write to the gnome to find out if he was pleased with them.

A week passed. They composed the letter, and the teacher promised to mail it. There was no answer. For three days the children rushed to school to see if the gnome's letter had arrived. At last, on the fourth day, the letter appeared.

All

> DEAR CHILDREN
>
> I HAVE BEEN SLEEPING BETTER LATELY.
> THANK YOU. I WOULD LIKE TO VISIT YOU.
> BUT I WILL NOT KNOW YOUR NAMES.
> WILL YOU DRAW ME A PICTURE OF YOURSELF
> WITH YOUR NAME ON IT AND SEND IT TO ME,
> PLEASE? ALSO TELL ME A DATE WHEN I
> CAN VISIT.
> YOURS SINCERELY **KNOBBLY**

The self-portraits were duly drawn and sent with a letter naming a day. The gnome replied that that day would be suitable. The children were very excited! What would he look like? How would he behave? Would he come by bus or what? They spent time tidying the room, doing paintings to brighten the walls, writing stores to read to him, etc.

The day before he was to come, when the children were in a fine state, this letter arrived:

> DEAR CHILDREN
>
> I **DON'T** WANT TO COME TOMORROW. I
> AM SCARED OF THE NOISE YOU MAKE. IF YOU
> CAN MAKE NICE NOISES, LIKE MONGS OR
> SOOZICK (I THINK THAT'S WHAT YOU CALL
> THEM) THEN I MIGHT CHANGE MY MIND.
> SORRY
> **KNOBBLY**

Great disappointment followed—but what were "mongs" and "soozick"? Nice noises? Ah! Songs and music! Over the next couple of days the children practiced two songs. Another letter was written to the gnome pleading with him to come on a new date and assuring him that he'd hear nice noises.

The gnome agreed.

DEAR CHILDREN

I AM COMING TOMORROW. IT IS THE BEST DAY FOR ME. I LOOK FORWARD TO HEARING YOUR MONGS. I SHALL KNOCK ON YOUR DOOR AT 11:15.

YOURS SINCERELY

KNOBBLY

Well, of course I arrived—dressed in leg warmers, an enormous moth-eaten sweater of my husband's, dark glasses, and a woolly hat pulled down over my forehead. I knocked on the door and the kids froze in ecstatic fright. I spoke in a deep voice:

"Is this Room Six? Then you must be my friends, right? Hmmm. What's your name? I forgot to bring your pictures. I have a terrible memory. What's your name? Hello everyone! Let's hear your mongs, then." I was gruff and grumpy.

The children sang their songs and then said they'd show me their classroom. I feigned total ignorance of everything. What's a story? I only write letters. What's this? A desk? I write on the floor. What's this? A blackboard? But it's green! And so on.

A party had been prepared and a conversation really got going, initiated by the teacher but soon taken up by the class. The children asked questions.

"How do you wash yourself in the ceiling at school?"

"Wash myself? What's 'wash'?"

The children, appalled, explained. They mentioned getting under the shower.

"Don't your clothes get wet?" I asked.

"No! You take them off!"

"All of them?" I said, shocked.

"Yes."

"Oh, how rude!" I said, and the children rolled with laughter.

"What do you eat?" asked the teacher.

"Eat? Eat? Cornflakes, of course. What else is there to eat?"

And the children, in high spirits, explained about the foods we eat—cakes, meat, vegetables, etc.

The teacher told the children to offer me some party food. I ate it with relish. (I truly love food!) My manners were disgusting. As I talked I let pieces of cupcake fall from my mouth in the most revolting manner. They told me that my manners were very bad.

In the end I had to go. I told them to watch me getting into my disguise. I took off my hat, dark glasses, sweater, and leg warmers and looked like me on an ordinary day.

"This is my disguise," I said. "Will anyone recognize me, do you think? My car is disguised. At the moment it looks like a yellow Toyota, license number SLF932. Actually, it's a pumpkin shell, drawn by a camel with wings. It's been lovely being here. Do write to me. I promise to answer every letter. See you!"

And off I went. What an incredible experience it was for all of us!

34 The Ghost from the Past

This happening was part of the Bachelor of Education drama methodology course of an ex-student of mine. I wanted to be in at the beginning, the middle, and the end to keep in touch with events.

I was invited to the school to tell stories—a normal occurrence. It was a class of mostly seven-year-olds. I told "The Golden Leg" (I don't know the source because I've only heard it; I've never read it) and "The Hand of Glory" from *Clever Gretchen and Other Forgotten Folk Tales* by Alison Lurie (New York: Crowell Junior Books, 1980). These stores set the scene because they were about the supernatural.

The classroom was a portable, prefabricated one, away from the main body of the school. It had a telephone in it. The principal had been asked to call at a certain time. As we talked about our favorite bits of the stories, the telephone rang. The teacher answered. Her side of the conversation went like this:

"I beg your pardon. Can you speak up? I can't hear a thing you're saying. Speak up! A ghost? Don't make me laugh! What? In our school? My class? Well, I'll have to ask them."

She looked at us in amazement and said to us: "I'll explain in a minute." Then she went on listening. "I see. Yes. I understand. Well, I can't promise, but I'll do my best."

The teacher then said, with eyes round with amazement: "That was a ghost. I'm not joking. He said he was 150 years old. His voice was weak—I could hardly get what he was saying. He wants our help. But he didn't have time to tell me anything except that the next message can be found in the school in a place that gets very, very hot. First, will we do it? I mean, will we help him?"

The children agreed. I forgot to say that the teacher had warned the kids for weeks that they were going to play a tremendous game of pretend one day—that it wouldn't be true, but that she would pretend that it was, and she hoped that they would too. One of the children whispered, "Is this it?" "Yes," the teacher whispered, "this is it."

A discussion followed about places in the school that were hot. We decided to try the incinerator. Sure enough, in the ashes was a map, burned on the edges. It was a map of the school and showed a particular clump of pine trees marked with an X. We moved towards it. One girl burst into tears and

Older

111

clung to my skirt. "I'm scared!" she said. I whispered that we were only pretending it was true, but I held her hand tightly anyway.

In the branches of one of the pine trees, a tape was discovered. We raced back to the classroom and played it. The voice on the tape said something to this effect:

> Hello, children. My name is Captain Perdix. I need your help. One hundred years ago I hid a box of pearls on the beach near your school. Then I was shipwrecked and I drowned. Those pearls are mine. One day I will give them to someone special.
>
> My problem is that Desperate Dan knows about them and is after them. I'd like you to try to trick him so that he can't find them.
>
> Desperate Dan is an antique dealer who wears a patch over his eye. Sometimes he dresses like a woman. Look out for any strange people around your school. I am too weak at the moment to move the pearls myself. Ghosts don't have much strength, you know. Do whatever you can. I shall contact you later. Goodbye.

I was a strange woman! "It's not me!" I said, and showed them my driver's license and my credit cards.

I left at that point, just as the class was discussing how to throw Desperate Dan off the scent.

The following day, every child in the class made a map—a different map, with "PEARLS" written on it and marked with an X. These they hid around the classroom to confuse Desperate Dan in case he came in.

During the week all the rulers mysteriously disappeared. Desperate Dan was thought to be the culprit. One of the children was asked to go around the school asking if anyone had seen a pile of rulers. One teacher had, of course, on her desk! What's more, her classroom had looked very strange when she'd come in—as if the desks had all been moved and some papers on her desk had been shifted. This news and the rulers were relayed back to the classroom. Excitement grew.

One very funny accidental thing happened. Electricians were called into the school for a genuine repair. As soon as the children saw them, they were all for capturing them and questioning them closely. Two of the boys had to be forcibly restrained by the teacher, who was nearly in hysterics!

Late one afternoon, when the children had gone home, the teacher moved the manhole cover in the ceiling so that there appeared to be a gaping hole. She said nothing. It took three days before a child looked dreamily upwards and then froze. "Miss! Miss! Look!" The class was agog. They decided to write to Captain Perdix to ask him to risk telling them where the pearls were. They wanted to hide them elsewhere, to put Desperate Dan off the track and to get him off their backs.

They longed for a reply. A child who had been very reluctant to come to school for the first two years of his school life made his mother drive him to school early, just in case a letter had arrived from Captain Perdix.

At this point, I was called in again. One afternoon, looking ridiculous in an old granny hat and with a patch over my eye, I allowed myself to be seen skulking near the classroom. There was no holding them this time! I ran like the wind away from the yelling mob and leapt over the school fence and into my car, which I started with a squeal of the tires. Fantastic fun! I felt exhilarated! The children were really in the game by now and were absolutely outraged.

The next day a letter from Captain Perdix arrived, telling the class where the pearls were and asking them to hide each one separately among the rocks on the northern end of the beach on the following morning.

I was asked to come with the class as extra protection in case Desperate Dan caused any trouble. On a cold Thursday morning we all went to the beach. There was a man on the jetty. A strange man! A real man! Nothing to do with Desperate Dan! The children insisted on getting closer to see if he had a patch over his eye. I was in stitches. It was terribly embarrassing— heaven knows what he thought we were all up to!

We searched among the rocks and found a beautifully carved box (mine). Inside it was a box of chocolates and a note in a spidery hand that read:

> Dear Children,
>
> Thank you for your help. My strength came back so I have hidden the pearls myself in a safe place far from here. The box of chocolates is my present to you. Desperate Dan is in jail for the rest of his life. He was caught stealing rulers at another school. Thank you very much for everything you have done.
>
> Goodbye and be good!
>
> Yours ever,
> Captain Perdix

We all went back to the classroom to eat chocolates and to talk about the whole experience from start to finish. Whew! Fantastic!

35 Queen Meany

This happening took place in a class where the children were terrific, but they weren't reading enough, according to their teacher. "You only learn to read by reading," she said, "and these kids rarely pick up a book."

For the whole of one week the teacher read three books a day to the children. (Not chapter books, of course.) On the following Monday a letter arrived, delivered by the school secretary, who said that a most peculiar woman had delivered it: she'd been wearing a cloak and a silly tinfoil crown.

A child opened the letter and they read it with the teacher's help. It said:

> Dear Children
>
> Books are STUPID. I hate them. I am going to DESTROY all the books in the world, starting at your SCHOOL. In two weeks all the books will be gone from the LIBRARY.
> You'll see! Ha Ha.
>
> Queen Meany.

A discussion followed in which the full implications of this threat were realized. What was the class to do? The teacher could read them more books, but really they'd have to try to read some themselves. They went straight to the library and told the librarian she'd better look out because Queen Meany was about to destroy all her books.

The librarian, who cooperated beautifully, was nearly driven

All

mad over the next week by children borrowing books.

Then another letter arrived.

DEAR CHildren

I feel sorry for you. If you tell me why books are important and show me what's in them I will not DESTROY every book.

I shall come to your school in ten days' time.

Queen Meany.

This letter was an opportunity for the teacher to encourage the class to try some drama activities in groups, related to the books they'd read. She said that the best way to show how important books were would be to act out something that would really please Queen Meany. They rehearsed for days.

On the appointed day I came into the classroom early, wearing red plastic glasses without glass, a tinfoil crown, and a long black cloak (my mother's graduation gown). I hid behind a curtain. The children came in noisily and I heard one say: "Aarrhh, she won't come," in a voice filled with scorn.

"Would you like to bet on that?" I said, and swept out grandly from behind the curtain. The looks on their faces nearly made me laugh, but I remained revoltingly stern and stared hard at a particular boy.

"Chair, boy," I said imperiously, and he obeyed without thinking or protesting.

"Well, you pathetic idiots! I know you've been reading books. I've peeped at you through the window. You silly things. Why read books? Why? Go on. I haven't got all day."

The children answered hesitantly because I was so horrible.

"Well!" I said. "Is that all you've got to say? It isn't good enough. Burn the books! Burn the books! I must be off. There will be no more books!"

At this point, the teacher restrained me and begged me to watch what the children had prepared. I cheered up and said: "Ah! Plays! I love a good play. Get on with it, then."

The plays were performed. At the end I praised them mightily and asked where they'd got their ideas from. "Books," they said.

"Books? Hmmm. In that case I shall have to have another think. I may change my mind. On the other hand, I may not. Wait and see. I shall write to you next week. Thank you and good day!'' I swept out.

Of course, a letter came saying that books seemed to be all right after all. But if the children stopped reading books, then books were clearly a waste of time after all and would be destroyed. So they read a lot of books! Hurrah!

36 The Witch Who Wouldn't Wake Up

In this happening a witch's cat appeals for help. She writes a
letter on a card shaped like a cat. She hangs the card on a string
in the doorway of the classroom, so that it hangs low enough
for five-year-olds to see as they come in from lunch.

Dear CHILDREN

I AM A WITCH'S CAT, and I'm
in trouble. My Mistress fell
asleep two days ago
and hasn't woken up
SINCE. I have licked her face
and miaowed in her ear but she just
goes on snoring. I think she drank
a sleeping spell, but I'm not sure. I did
see a mean old WITCH called WIGGUMS
creeping about last week. Perhaps she
cast a spell on my mistress. I don't know
what to do.
Can you suggest something?

YOURS SINCERELY.
CHRISTOPHER.

P.S. THE NAME OF MY MISTRESS IS Miss WINTER.

All

As I write this, I have ideas such as all the class getting into a circle and yelling, "Wake up, Miss Winter!" at the top of their voices. Or Wiggums appearing briefly in the classroom and telling the children to stop meddling. Or making spells and incantations and writing them out for Christopher to chant. However, the glorious thing about happenings is that teachers don't have to come up with their own ideas if they listen carefully enough to the children in their class. Children are much more imaginative than we are at times like this and should be heavily relied upon to provide the tension and momentum in any happening. Try it and see.